Number 2
LANE MORGAN, *Editor*

The Northwest Experience

SEATTLE • *Madrona Publishers* • 1981

Grateful acknowledgment is made to the following for permission to print copyrighted material:

Bruce Brown for "Wild Salmon," from *Mountain in the Clouds: A Search for the Wild Salmon.* © 1981 by Bruce Brown.

Norman H. Clark and Harper & Row, Publishers, Inc. for "James G. Swan." © 1969 by Harper & Row, Publishers, Inc., as the introduction to *The Northwest Coast, or Three Years' Residence in Washington Territory,* by James G. Swan.

Ivan Doig and Harcourt Brace Jovanovich, Inc. for "Gone West," from *Winter Brothers.* © 1980 by Ivan Doig.

Steve Forrester and *Willamette Week* for "Tom McCall," originally published in the May 16, 1977 issue of *Willamette Week* as "Will Tom McCall run again?" © 1977 by *Willamette Week.*

Hazel Heckman and the University of Washington Press for "Island Imports," from *Island in the Sound.* © 1967 by the University of Washington Press.

Greg Hill for *Energy 1990.* © 1981 by Greg Hill.

Doug Honig and *Seattle Sun* for "Victor Steinbrueck," originally published in a shorter form as "Planning for Lovers and Friends" in the May 14, 1980 issue of *Seattle Sun.*

E. Kimbark MacColl for "Bonneville," from *The Growth of a City: Power and Politics in Portland, Oregon, 1915 to 1950,* The Georgian Press. © 1979 by E. Kimbark MacColl.

Harvey Manning for "Walking the Beach," from *Walking the Beach to Bellingham.* © 1981 by Harvey Manning.

Rick Rubin for "Coyote on the Columbia," from *Barefoot in Rainy Eden.* © 1981 by Rick Rubin.

Richard White and the University of Washington Press for "The Farmer on the Land," from *Land Use, Environment, and Social Change: The Shaping of Island County, Washington.* © 1980 by the University of Washington Press.

Steve Woodruff and *Willamette Week* for "Timber in Oregon," originally published in the June 2, 1980 edition of *Willamette Week* as "Exporting Timber: Jobs Across the Sea." © 1980 by *Willamette Week.*

Published by
Madrona Publishers, Inc.
2116 Western Avenue
Seattle, Washington 98121

The Northwest Experience:

THINKING REGIONALLY IS harder to do than I thought two years ago when we began collecting material for this series. It is easier to make the jump from the intimate concerns of family and neighborhood to an all-encompassing nationalism than it is to be a citizen of the Pacific Northwest.

For me, the *real* Northwest is a strip of western Washington from the site of my great-grandparents' oyster farm on southern Puget Sound to the dairy-farming community on the Canadian border where I now live. This strip encompasses the formerly rural, now suburban neighborhood where I grew up, and Seattle, where I lived for several years.

This is a small and comparatively homogeneous part of the Northwest, but even it is diverse enough to challenge attempts at synthesis. My present neighbors wonder how anyone could bear to live in Seattle, and I can only try to imagine my great-grandmother's Northwest, a cabin in deep woods where she raised seven children while her husband hunted Klondike gold.

Whether we take it for granted as the only world we know, or whether we like it best because it isn't New Jersey, our personal Northwest is always the most vivid. It is our starting point. A regional perspective begins with individual experience. We need to know who we are and why we are here before we can talk sensibly about what we want to become.

The Northwest Experience is a place to voice these individual Northwests. Our job is not to be first on the newsstands with the latest idea, but to foster an extended conversation among compatriots who are separated by time and territory.

Out of this exchange may come some sensible proposals for regional policy. We might find that the most persuasive blending of individual rights and mass strength comes at the regional level. I hope so.

The conversation continues outside of the pages of this book. In particular I would like to thank the staff of the University of Washington Press and Steve Johnson and E. Kimbark MacColl of Portland for their suggestions and encouragement.

LANE MORGAN

Contents

The Northwest Experience

Walking the Beach

HARVEY MANNING

This is an excerpt from Walking the Beach to Bellingham, *a manuscript in progress scheduled for publication in 1982 by Madrona Publishers. Harvey Manning, author of* Footsore, Walks and Hikes around Puget Sound, *volumes 1 through 4, and a number of other works on hiking and mountaineering, is a native of Ballard. He now lives in the Issaquah Alps east of Seattle.*

Picnic Point to Edmonds   *Mile 28-22*
Friday, April 2, 1976

2:30. Kill off the Pepsi Cola, stomp the can and stuff it in the rucksack with the kipper can. Toss apple core to the gulls to see the flapping and squawking. Turn south toward faraway turrets shimmering in haze, the Silver City on Edwards Point.

Between seawall and incoming tide a narrow beach was still open, and when all is said and done, sand and cobbles are happier walking than tracks. The eye-stinging reek of creosoted ties is as haunting to an old beach bum as low-tide stink, but the salt smell is primordial, the memory flows in our blood.

I walked under the sagging wharf at Norma Beach, the outer brightness the more dazzling from the darkness of the piling forest.

The beach pinched out and I climbed the seawall. Three-point suspension, weight over feet, test holds, climb with the eyes — even as on the South Face of The Tooth, the awful wall of Bruiser Cruiser, the Northwest Ridge of Sir Donald. I sat on my summit, feet dangling over water, and ate a Three Musketeers.

The sugar power was wanted, the miles were growing long. But good.

At Meadowdale Beach the mellow lads offered the bearded old man a beer, only half in derision. He genially declined, having many miles to go before he'd drink. I used to pity the ragged old men, lower than hoboes, perhaps tramps or even bums, shambling along the tracks as they had since the Railroad Trails were built. But it's not so bad being a ragged old man shambling along the tracks. One might be, instead, a clean old man in suit and white shirt and tie, wasting the brightness building airplanes for Boeing.

Rounding a bulge I looked back and saw I'd lost the magic islet of Picnic Point in haze. Two hours buried in the past. But not lost. None of it was lost, the past was eternal and everywhere and only wanted the walking to be found. Nor was there pain in the finding. I'd thought so, had shunned the past, dreading its growing mass measured against a shrinking future. Yet the mass was wealth. Each day I was richer and today I'd gained many treasures — Meadowdale Beach and Lunds Gulch and Picnic Point. And the day stretched endlessly ahead.

A ferry was docking. I sat on the seawall and ate an apple. The tide, having swallowed the beach, was climbing the wall. Choppy waves stirred by a rising breeze slapped the granite blocks.

5:06, the ferry pulled out. Boys in a sailing catamaran slid swiftly by the shore. Huge black fish broke the waves, rose up on hind legs and strode from the primordial, wetsuits glistening. A lad was sleeping on the seawall.

Trip's end. I climbed from tracks to lawns atop the low bank, sat on a park bench beside my Beetle, and stretched legs. 5:12, open a can of beer. The thirst from twelve miles and six sunshine hours instantly vaporized the long, chill, nose-tingling, eye-tearing, half-quart swallow. Light as a bubble the mind floated up from the clay, bright as the sun a glow from within illuminated inner and outer worlds. It was revealed that *this was the moment it all was for*. After decades of patches and fidgets, false starts and dead ends, signifying nothing, I was free to walk about the countryside in all the beautiful places and ask the important question: "Where did I come from?" I could leave others to ask themselves the trivial question: "Where am I going?"

In returning south I'd regained the window on the Seven Seas. I'd never go. I was a creature of the Inland Sea, guarded by mountains from the vastness sloping to the brink of the void. I needed Olympics west and Cascades east to lean against, lest I fall down.

To be sure, now and then I ventured to the Great Plains specifically for the giddiness of the Big Sky, and understood why its people become claustrophobic on the Inland Sea. And frequently I dared the dragon coast where no mountain wall bounds the imagination, where giant waves roar of frightening matters.

But to go out from shore . . . . As avidly as once I read Masefield and Conrad I now pored over letters from a friend in the merchant marine, and loved his tales of mama-sans, typhoons, and saloon brawls in steaming seaports, and envied him the exotic nations of the gorgeous postage stamps. Yet I felt more akin to a landlubber friend who once, to keep his rendezvous with a childhood dream, set off on a voyage around the world. Soon appalled, he retreated to his cabin whenever the ship left sight of land and kept the steward on the run bringing gin to dull the horror.

My longest sea journey was in 1945, on the Canadian Pacific's *Princess* boat that left Seattle in early morning, docked in Victoria at noon, returned in evening. We voyaged down the Sound to Admiralty Inlet, to the Strait of Juan de Fuca, and over the broad gulf to the foreign nation where steak-and-kidney pie was on the menu, the cigarettes were Players and Black Cats, the "ou" dipthong was mispronounced, and retired British majors in mustaches and tweeds bicycled around the rose gardens.

5:20, the sun was high above the blue Olympic silhouette in a yellow cirrus sky. A freight train passed, the sound of discipline, the nineteenth century, different from the noise of simian chaos, the twentieth century. Man can live beside a railroad, not by a freeway nor under an airway.

5:30, a ferry coming in. Open beer #2.

5:37, a freight going south — and simultaneously, another north! Wow-ee! It struck me there'd been more traffic than usual all day. Like olden times. I remembered — the Teamsters were on strike, and may they stay on the bricks until their wheels turn square.

The Inland Sea had a sane and happy transportation system, the mosquito fleet, and killed it with Model Ts and As and Mack and Kenworth trucks, and now America was slaughtering its rail network with freeways and airways. The "railroad" companies were focusing their greed on plundering their stolen land grants. To do so the more efficiently they were mergerizing toward an ultimate One Big Non-Railroad Company. However, though only the polysynthetic Burlington Northern survived now on the shores of Puget Sound, the wooden walls of passing trains preserved such old boasts as "Northern Pacific, Route of the Vista Dome North Coast Limited," and displayed Great Northern's mountain goat that in nights of yore shone electrically bright in the downtown Seattle sky. Other boxcars spoke of the rails that linked the continent: Chicago, Milwaukee, and St. Paul; Atchison, Topeka and Santa Fe; Southern Pacific, Union Pacific, Rock Island Line, Pennsy, New York Central, B&O, C&O, B&M.

The sport of peasant boys was counting the cars of freights, waving to engineer and fireman in heroic black engine and brakeman in cozy red caboose. But passenger trains were our drama, windows flashing by with a blur of faces, the golden people of Hollywood movies, the nobility of the Mysterious East, citizens of skyscrapers, taxicabs, penthouses, night clubs and luxury liners, the bright lights of the permanent party.

There was my future. But when at last I was summoned East the nation had been Boeinged, Douglassed, Lockheeded. The airplanes that noised the sky had shrunk the planet, giving the ahistorical specious adventures, the ageographical false perspectives on lands and seas.

A plumbers' convention in Schenectady, Aunt Sally's goiter operation in Fresno, steak sandwiches with a fertilizer manufacturer in Houston, a swim in a pool in Omaha, a slot machine in Reno, a fruit salad in Honolulu, are solemnized by the passage through air. Thinking by altitude to achieve significance, by massing of miles to fill empty lives, the mobs herd into airports and are swindled. Docks were thrilling and train stations exciting, airports are simply saddening.

I once managed to evade the airplane by taking the Canadian National from Vancouver. We journeyed through the Fraser River Canyon (my route to the British Columbia Coast Range and a close view of Mount Waddington) and past mighty Mount Robson (whose summit I plotted against) and over Alberta parklands and Saskatchewan prairies. A lord of the realm, I walked the swaying corridor to the dining car, the silver and white linen, the sumptuous napkin folded in a pyramid, the crystal goblet wherein water jiggled and ice cubes clinked, the slice of chill melon with a twist of lemon, the lambchops with mint sauce and panties. Before retiring to my roomette I sat in the club car and watched the Canadian night roll by and drank a McEwan's Strong.

By train, too — the Canadian Pacific — we traveled in 1950 to the Selkirks to climb Mount Sir Donald and gaze over the white vastness of the Illecilleweet Névé. The same August, while four of us were rappelling in darkness off the North Peak of Index after the hottest day of the summer, canteens dry for hours, dusty throats glueing shut, breath coming in rasping gasps, I stared a vertical mile down through night to the Great Northern passenger train gliding beside the Skykomish River, and saw the shining windows and thought of the golden people within and all the water they were drinking.

5:45, the ferry out. 5:50, open beer #3. 6:00, another ferry in. The street behind my beach was filling with parked cars. The sun was about two inches above Marmot Pass, where in 1938 I first saw wilderness. In a sunset. My first Parsons hike.

The morning after that sunset we traversed Dungeness head-waters to Home Lake, a droplet of ice water beneath eastern cliffs of Mount Constance, and all afternoon I gazed in awe up the ramparts, wondering if they'd ever been climbed.

Due west four and a half miles over Main Street, Appletree Point. In the spring of 1940 Troop 324 walked on the ferry at Ed-monds, from Kingston hiked north on the beach and camped at the point in abandoned buildings. That summer I twice followed the crest of Lost Ridge, one day in sunshine and wind, gazing west to glaciers of Mount Olympus, the next in a screaming Three Day Blow. My last Parsons hike.

I and Appletree Point and Marmot Pass were in a straight line; extended west through hidden Olympics it would intersect Lost Ridge, and west more, Olympus, which fell to my boots in 1949.

South of Marmot Pass, Constance, apex of the Olympic sky-line. With ax in hand and rope on waist I stood there in 1948 and looked to *here*.

Farther south, The Brothers, 1949. In sunsets like this, in 1856, the coast surveyor George Davidson sat on the porch of his sweetheart's Seattle home looking over Puget Sound to the peaks, naming them for her family. I couldn't distinguish his sweetheart's mountain, Ellinor, near the south end of the range, but big sister Constance was plain, and the two boys.

6:05, #4. Milk-blue crags and ridges outlined against smoke-yellow sky. Wizened red ball radiating five long sunrays to the ends of the sky, a wonder often portrayed, as on the flag of Japan, but seldom seen. Few people watch a sunset all the way.

6:13, the ferry out.

Let it go, let them all go today, there'll be more tomorrow and I'll be on them. Too long I've neglected my ferries. The present is a night-haunted misery, the future is for the fools and villains who are making it and deserve it, all I want is the past, a ferry-boat, and a can of beer.

6:20, #5, *Rainier* beer, of course. I climbed this can! Never sailed the small boat around the world, never climbed Everest, but in 1948 (and '49 and '50 and '51 and '52) I climbed this beer can and was 14,416 feet tall.

6:25, sun entering the horizon, having drifted north from Marmot Pass beyond Mount Townsend, where in 1946 we climbed from Windy Lakes on a breakfast of stewed apricots and met Whiskers Jack Conrad, who lived alone a year in Montana wilderness, never seeing a soul, and when he came out to Missoula felt real bashful walking the streets and had the notion folks were staring at him, and thought maybe he had a hole in the seat of his britches, so began feeling around back there as he walked, and got surer and surer folks were staring.

The sun was slipping in just a couple inches from the north end of the range, where behind foreground ridges lay Blue Mountain, hidden. From its summit on a summer night in 1946 I looked down to twinkling Sequim and over twenty black miles of the Straight of Juan de Fuca to the constellation of Victoria.

This sun, this skyline, this Main Street, all these I knew of old. Though the land I'd walked today was somewhat more battered and torn, water and sky were the same. And so was I. In the mirror of the past shone the inner constant.

6:30. There goes the sun.

I am not alone. Street and park strip and beach are crowded, silent. Sunset-watchers. Past-watchers. The hope (if any) of the world.

Picnic Point to Mukilteo   Mile 28-33
Tuesday, April 27, 1976

The unknown. A shore with no memories. And though I'd given up the freedom of ignorance to web with maps, their primitive language could no more express all the variations of land and water than a nose whistle could a Beethoven quartet. There would be surprises.

Barely a mile beyond Picnic Point, a hybrid delta-sandspit, was a true spit, a pure spit, larger than Picnic Point and with all the proper parts, even a lagoon.

And more. Snuggled in a poplar grove was a cottage as weathered as the beachcomber's treasures around it in the sand — driftwood sculptures, fishing nets and floats, rotten rowboats become flower planters. In the breeze atop a pole waved Old Glory, as innocently patriotic as Commodore Bainbridge's squadron showing the flag in ports of the Barbary States. No electricity or telephone wires led in, and no road. A home for an old salt turning his back on wheels and TV and land, gazing out to sea.

Still more! Ghosts of wooden ships and white sails, lumber schooners and mosquito fleet. Presumably this, like Richmond Beach, was the scene of stripping and burning. Two rib cages poked through the sands. But also, beached to rot on a strand between waves and lagoon, was a complete hull.

For a high perspective on "Shipwreck Spit" I climbed beside the cottage's water supply, a tumbling creek, on a staircase cut in clay 260 feet through forest to the bluff top. I started slow but suddenly found myself running up the stairs, forty pounds the nimbler since the Great Reform Act. Then down I ran, hickory dickory dock.

This morning I'd awakened unrested and jangled from cigarette nightmares — white tubes that materialized unwanted in fingers and lips, butts that black-magically overflowed ashtrays, coals that burned rugs and clothes, smoke that blinded and strangled. I couldn't sit a desk until the afternoon walk that had been part of my daily routine since March 12. I had to be off, needed a full day of the metronome.

Running up and down the bluff at Shipwreck Spit put me back on the track. I strode long-legged north between green bluff and white surf — not Mr. Manic yet well-escaped from Dorian Gray. A fellow rolled by on a speeder. We exchanged waves and smiles. A wind from the north cooled my face, cleared morning veils from the Olympics, the sun, and the blue, bringing the promised brightness. In cattails of a trackside ditch the redwing blackbirds rasped, frogs croaked.

North from behind a bulge appeared a ferry westering to Whidbey Island. I looked back south and beyond the Poplar Isle of Picnic Point saw a ferry westering from the Silver City. I turned north again and saw a ferry eastering from Whidbey.

Yo ho ho, the wind blows free!
Oh for the life on the In-n-n-land Sea!

But scoundrels had been here, chainsawing the bluff wilderness into a jackstraw of fallen logs and tangled slash to open the view for new homes atop the bluff. Up there 120 feet the map showed "Chenault Beach Road." But no road descended to the beach, nor even a trail, and indeed there was no beach. Scoundrels indeed, frauds and assassins.

Yet just past the carnage was peace — Big Gulch, shown by the map as slicing the drift plateau one-and-a-half miles inland to Paine Field. Wide, deep and wild. But not a park, though there was the Olympic Terrace Sewage Plant. (Picnic Point also was Worthied, I'd learned driving down its creek valley today, finding there the Alderwood Manor Wastewater Treatment Plant.)

I entered the gulch to scowl at the Worthy Cause. The manager came out to smile at me. My scowl was defeated. He was only incidentally the resident attendant. His true vocation was ranger, guarding a wildlife sanctuary from poachers and midnight loggers. The valley was uninhabited, the entry road closed to the public, he was the only human here and rarely had a visitor. He told of coots and mallards and goldeneyes and buffleheads, scaups and cormorants and wigeons, mobs of a thousand gulls offshore at the sewage outfall, fleets of many thousands of migratory waterfowl swimming by at sea. He told of sandpipers and killdeer on the beach, choirs of forest birds and creek birds, and bald eagles perched on snags, harassed by gangs of crows. He told of seals in the waves and weasels on the sand, and deer and bear that paid him no more mind than they did each other.

This was a Cause Worthier than most. Paine Field was built when "environmental impact" was still called "progress" and none objected to the Army Air Corps dumping raw sewage in Big Gulch to run in the open to the delta. The later burying of the sewer line in the creek bed hadn't destroyed a creek because there wasn't any. But now there was, clean and loud in new-growing forest, delight of birds and beasts and the Ranger.

A noisome past had been repaired. The future? Only a half-dozen homes had been built since platting of Chenault "Beach" in 1942. But overnight the sewage plant had raised the selling price of lots from $400 to $15,000. The boom was on. And what about the bears and the eagles?

1942. Yes, that was the start.

At the onset of the Depression the newly poor fled city taxes and bureaucracy and laws for the freedom of the country, which offered no piped water, no sewers, no garbage trucks, no fire protection, few police, and roads that were mud in winter and washboard in summer. There in "the country" a family could borrow space on a friend's property, scavenge scrap lumber for a tarpaper shack, dig one hole for a well and another for a privy, cut firewood in second-growth forests nobody owned, raise chickens and grow potatoes and corn and peas. When times got better, the land could be bought for a hundred bucks or so, electricity brought in to replace the kerosene. The well-off folks down the road had a telephone they let neighbors use in emergencies.

Adjoining the city were no suburbs, only a narrow fringe of city limits slum just beyond reach of higher taxes and stiffer laws. Then, all the way to the next city, pure country, inter-rupted by the scattering of old, tight-knit, sharply-defined towns — Richmond Beach, Edmonds, Meadowdale.

1942. The cure for Depression had been found. Platting, dead since the Crash, resumed. Fields and forests were staked and ribboned for weekend Victory Gardens.

V-J Day. Lumber and carpenters came home from the war. Vegetable gardens were covered by ranch ramblers and lawns. Beach trails were closed off. My backyard wilderness was logged. Commerce oozed north and south on highway shoulders to form 99 Strip City. Seattle merged into Edmonds, and Edmonds into Mukilteo and Everett, the gaps filled by instant synthetic cities — Mountlake Terrace, Alderwood Manor, Lynnwood.

In 1947 my folks sold the house and moved to Oregon. In disgust and horror, I ejected the old neighborhood from my thoughts. What was happening there unsettled reason, violated laws of nature. In school they'd taught us that the population of the United States, 131,669,275 in 1940, up merely from 122,775,046 in 1930, would top out in the twenty-first century at 150,000,000, followed by the natural decline normal for a civilized nation. But the population in 1950 was already 150,697,361, and in 1960 was 179,323,175, grossly unnatural, insane, obscene, and there go the bears and the eagles, there goes country.

Standing on the tip of the Big Gulch Delta I pondered a Momentous Geographic Event. At day's start I'd looked over three miles of Main Street to Possession Point, the tip of Whidbey Island. Now I was around the corner, up the alley. The Olympics were falling away south, already unfamiliar in this perspective.

I was beyond Puget Sound, was on Possession Sound.

Tom McCall

STEVE FORRESTER

This article originally appeared in the May 16, 1977 issue of Willamette Week *under the title "Will Tom McCall run again?" McCall, who served two terms as governor of Oregon, starting in 1967, did run again in 1978. He lost to Victor Atiyeh in the primary.*

Steve Forrester is a former managing editor of Willamette Week. *Since 1978 he has been an independent Washington correspondent for Northwest newspapers. He is a native of Pendleton.*

Tom McCall openly entertains the possibility that he will run again for governor in 1978.

And why shouldn't he? A poll published by *The Oregonian* last winter revealed McCall's popularity remains immensely high over two years after his second term as governor of Oregon ended. The poll indicated that in an election held between McCall and Gov. Bob Straub, McCall would win handily.

McCall's popularity is phenomenal. A national research organization, polling in Portland in January 1976, one year after his term ended, discovered that, "Tom McCall has one of the highest feeling thermometer scores we have ever measured for a political figure. Mr. McCall would have to be considered an extremely formidable candidate for any office he should choose to seek."

Just as the memory of McCall's colorful administration is hardening into legend, speculation is rife that he will take another run at the office he was forced by the constitutional limit of two terms to depart.

McCall's ego and character give rise to the kinds of speculation wafting about. McCall not only is one of the best shows in the state, he remains a legend.

But legends are often best left alone, so this story perhaps bears the seeds of tragedy. And despite the enormity of McCall's ego, this story has a very human dimension, because today the man yearns for center stage and the huge doses of ego feed high elective office provides. "It's hard to disengage once you've been drinking that oxygen," says a friend of McCall's.

I. WILL TOM RUN?

Tom McCall seems to be going through withdrawal from the ego feed and emotional high of being a very popular governor. Sitting on a bright-yellow couch in the sunlit living room of his home on Broadway Drive in Portland Heights, McCall says, "The winding down can be grisly. It really can. What you miss is the organization of the office, the team. That whole relationship was something that was very precious to me, and very valuable to the state."

McCall is still that immensely engaging, likable, egocentric creature with the broad smile which involves the whole lantern jaw. But he is also frequently short of breath. Every now and then his concentration wanes and his mind wanders. He moves slowly, getting up and sitting down, and frequently puts his hands to his face and rubs his eyes.

"My health is good," he says. "I passed my cancer test." (McCall was operated on for cancer of the prostate during his second term.) But his mind seems dogged by three concerns: The television and radio commentaries he must write and deliver; the ongoing trauma caused by the problems of his son, Sam; and the tantalizing encouragement to run for governor he receives from Oregonians.

The former governor leads an arduous professional life. He turns out eleven commentaries each week — five for television and six for radio — plus doing a Sunday television show. His

TV commentaries are seen on four stations in Oregon, his radio pieces heard on five.

A newsman comments on the contradiction between McCall's nature and his present role. "He's not a disciplined individual. His spontaneity is one of his charms, and he's thrown himself into a schedule which demands discipline."

Watching McCall do his television commentary in the KATU-TV (Channel 2) studio, one feels a twinge of pathos. He does the job well, but the role does not become his stature or public esteem.

But one also notices that in the television studio McCall moves more quickly, with more purpose. During his commentary he pours out tremendous amounts of energy—his jaw thrust forward, moving fast.

McCall came to KATU after a short teaching stint at Oregon State University (OSU). Before he left public office, a number of Oregon business people contributed a large amount of money to OSU to endow a chair in politics and communications for him to occupy. But the job didn't work. "It was too static," McCall says. "Static means you gave your best speeches and they never clapped."

Sam McCall, the former governor's son, has suffered from drug and alcohol problems for a number of years. During his governorship, McCall and Sam participated in an NBC News special on drug abuse. McCall is remarkably candid about his son's problems. He says he owes between $7,000 and $8,000 in related hospital bills.

It's not surprising that McCall's mind is tired from the pressures of meeting deadlines—"God, I've worked hard all my life. I really have." And he is deeply worried about and loyal to his son—"We went all the way with him, sink or swim."

But beyond his worries, McCall basically is not a whole person—not truly alive, one suspects, without some dream of a return to elective office. "It's just remarkable what a romance there is between the old governor and the people. People are always saying, 'You've got to run.' This is not just 20 per cent or 70 per cent. This is *everybody* saying, 'You've got to go down there.'

"It's a hard thing for Straub, as it was for William Howard Taft, coming after Teddy Roosevelt."

Bob Davis, who was McCall's executive assistant during his second administration, says, "I don't know of anybody who enjoyed being governor of Oregon as much as he did. I remember sitting in the office, late one night after settling a strike. He looked across the desk and said, 'God, Bob, isn't this fun?'"

But McCall understands that he must be very cool and correct in whatever dreaming he allows himself, because once he becomes a candidate (declared or not) he goes off the air and is out of a job. "I haven't proceeded on it at all," he says. "It's dangerous. I've got a call here from a guy who wants to raise money for me. A guy came in yesterday and offered to raise $200,000. He said, 'Would that induce you to run?' I told him, 'You never saw me.'"

Money would certainly be a factor if McCall chose to run. The campaign involves about an eight-month stretch without money. McCall says he'd have to sell his Portland Heights home in order to eat during the campaign. But Ron Schmidt, McCall's former press secretary, says, "I don't think money would be a particular problem. I see money from past supporters, Democrats, liberal Republicans and Independents."

Thaddeus Bruno, a senior vice-president with the Gilley Co., and McCall's main fund-raiser in 1970, says, "I've left it this way with Tom. If he'd return to public life, I'd help him. He'd have a blank check with me. It seems a shame he's not back in the mainstream of public life, and a decision by him to do that would be most welcome."

Now that it has withstood challenges in court, McCall is eligible for the $18,000-per-year governor's pension, and it is cumulative in value. He has told friends he won't take the pension because the public would figure he's through if he did.

Part of what built the McCall legend was not simply McCall's splendid stage presence, but the staff he assembled.

John Mosser, McCall's first Revenue Department head, points out, "The people who campaigned for him and worked in his administration have all gone on to other things. McCall really has to put together another organization to campaign and run the government, and I don't know whether he'll do that."

One of those former McCall staffers is Ed Westerdahl, whom McCall has referred to as "the youngest father a 55-year-old guy ever had." McCall has told friends it was Westerdahl who took him in tow and enforced discipline on him in his 1964 run for secretary of state. Westerdahl says, "I've said to him that, for his interest and the interest of the family, he shouldn't run."

Schmidt, now Westerdahl's partner in a Portland advertising-public-relations firm, says, "I'm telling Tom that you can't go home again. He served eight very exciting years as governor, and he should have that as his record and not run again.

"I'm in close touch with the Carter administration. If Tom makes a decision that he'd like to have a major policy role in the Carter administration, it will be forthcoming."

Davis says, "My advice is that he's got to do what's best for Tom McCall personally."

Some say McCall's decision will be based on who else challenges Straub. Others suggest it will be entirely a matter of McCall's need to run.

In the Democratic Party, Portland Mayor Neil Goldschmidt has said he won't challenge Straub. Most often mentioned as a Democratic challenger is Jason Boe, president of the state Senate, but he does not seem impressive as a statewide candidate. In the Republican party, Sen. Victor Atiyeh is expected to make another run, and Rep. Roger Martin of Lake Oswego is talked about. Atiyeh, a good man, but lacking color, lost badly to Straub in 1974. Of the McCall possibility Atiyeh says, "Tom was a great governor. That may very well be the best role he can fulfill — as the conscience of the state for future governors. If he ran again and won, I have no doubt he could serve again as a great governor. But it may very well be he could continue his role with greater influence from the outside, rather than inside."

An interesting Republican possibility is Secretary of State Norma Paulus, who stated during her campaign that she would serve a full four years in that position before attempting higher office. One Republican insider, "Tuck" Wilson, assistant state treasurer, says, "The only one who could give McCall a run is Norma, not Roger Martin, who entered into a coalition with conservative Democrats last week."

Of the governor's race, Paulus says, "I've told Tom McCall that if he'd run, I'd support him."

The most critical support for McCall *Willamette Week* has discovered is among key liberal Democrats who say they are fed up with Straub and have encouraged McCall to run and have offered him their support.

Tougher Straub

Recently, Straub has taken a tougher stance toward the McCall possibility. He told a Corvallis town hall meeting last week, "McCall loves to run. He ran against Hatfield for the Senate. He ran against Packwood for the Senate until the last minute. Now it's my turn to be the focal point. He loves the tease. He loves to keep people on the edge of their seats."

Of Straub's performance, McCall told *Willamette Week*, "I don't know if news conferences and waving your arms is leadership."

An intriguing possibility is that of McCall running for governor as an Independent candidate, which would give voters a three-way choice in November 1978. Because of a law passed by the 1975 legislature, if McCall wants to do that, he must change his registration from Republican to Independent in September, six months before filing day.

In any event, McCall's role as commentator is sure to become an issue before filing day. Section 315 of Federal Communications Commission regulations, the "equal time" provision, requires that if McCall were a candidate, KATU-TV and KEX radio would have to put other gubernatorial candidates on every time McCall did his commentary.

"FCC law is clear on when a man becomes a candidate," says KEX General Manager Richard Kale. "A legally qualified candidate is publicly announced and meets the qualifications. At such time he is a declared candidate, he's out of a job. McCall has in no way indicated to me he would be a candidate."

Skip Hinman, KATU assistant general manager, says if McCall became a candidate, "He'd immediately cease being on the air." When does he become a candidate? "When he files," answers Hinman. What if a committee were raising money for McCall and organizing a campaign? "We would have to take a very serious look at it," replies Hinman.

McCall, who is 64, enjoys talking about the possibility of a return to office. "I know I could be a good governor again, because I've got the one thing that's vital — the support of the people. The second thing is putting together the staff. I'd be a better governor because I've been chastened by being on the outside."

Perhaps the most realistic assessment of whether McCall will run deals with McCall's character and drive. Ancil Payne, president of King Broadcasting, was station manager of KGW-TV when McCall was its commentator. "Anyone who looked at Tom leaving OSU and didn't recognize he's running is a dumbo," says Payne. "I don't think there's any question about it. It's his thing. These guys are like bulls in the bullring."

An old friend of McCall's sees it this way: "There are some persons who are just made for public life. They have it in spades. They make egregious errors sometimes, but they are so grand and their conceptions are so deep and their articulative powers are such that they overcome it. So Tom will run all of his life. Won't he? Of course he will!"

II. WHAT MAKES TOM RUN?

Ken Kesey might have invented Tom McCall: A man with an ego as big as the ranch he grew up on — spawned by exotic New

England lineage and childhood in a desolate but beautiful corner of Central Oregon.

Tom McCall is of Eastern Oregon, more properly of Central Oregon, but in any event he hails from that two-thirds of the state which is not damp and dense with forest and green vegetation. He is one of few Oregon governors to have come from that arid region, where his father was a rancher. Mark Hatfield is of the Willamette Valley — his father was a blacksmith — and he represents the Protestant-missionary strain of Oregon history. Bob Straub grew up in Los Angeles, where his father was legal counsel to Pacific Gas & Electric.

The valley where McCall grew up is one of the few places in Oregon which has not been freewayed or franchised into a place you might find in a number of other American locations. It is one of the most particular places in the state. The wind is your constant companion in this region of flat land, brush and scrub trees. When it dies down, there is immense quiet. When someone fires a rifle in these parts, the shot echoes down ravines and through gullies for a long time. The place can produce great emptiness or great fullness of heart.

One is closer to the elements here, and the people who live in this kind of place tend to be more elemental. If you respond to landscape, this stark, dry region will affect you. The sparseness of population and landscape gives a clear, sharp delineation to the persons one encounters. And, perhaps in answer to the loneliness, this region has produced more than its share of great, colorful characters.

Rimrock ranch

The three-story McCall ranch house, near the little town of Terre Bonne, is one of the wonders of Oregon. Built in 1911, it has a New England exterior of shutters and high-sloping roof, and a Western interior, with low ceilings, exposed beams and a broad, deep, front porch. A local resident, whose face and neck are red from work in the recent sunny days, looks at the house and says, "Hell, that's no ranch house. That's a castle."

The three-story house appears small, set under a high rimrock. It looks toward another rimrock across a flat valley, through which a river and a creek flow. Through the eastern end of the valley you can sight the ridge of Blue Mountains; through the western end, the Three Sisters of the Cascades.

The McCall ranch house is little changed from what it was like when the five McCall children were growing up. "Time has almost stopped at that ranch, particularly in the nursery," says a McCall family member. Hanging on pegs in the nursery are little leather boxing gloves and children's Indian headdresses. Dolls and toys are here and there. In the center of the room are large stuffed animals on wheels, big enough for children to ride — an elephant, bear, horse, camel, giraffe, lion and bison. The animals were sent to the McCall children by their immensely wealthy maternal grandfather, Thomas K. Lawson, the "Copper King."

On the second-floor landing of the house hangs a row of large photographs of the five McCall children as babies, being held by the mustached, distinguished "Copper King," who made this ranch house, called Westernwold, a gift to his daughter, Dorothy Lawson McCall.

Dreamy world

McCall was born at his grandfather's Cape Cod estate, Dreamwold, on whose veranda Hal McCall and Dorothy Lawson had been married one day in December. A snow wedding, it was called, as great wisps of snow fell on the glass-enclosed porch.

As a boy McCall returned to Dreamwold a number of times with his mother for visits. "Dreamwold — all of it — was still essentially there," he has written, "with its sweeping terraces and gardens, acres of handsome buildings and the fleet of limousines that would bear us to private school at Hingham, complete with chauffeur and footman and 'Granddaddy' spinning tales in the back to assorted grandchildren."

McCall and his siblings are a family almost overwhelmed by family history, so rich and deep is their lineage. "He's lived in the shadows of grandparents for years," says a former associate, "and his political success moved him out of it. But once that process of living in the shadows starts, it's hard to slip out for good."

Probably the most dominant personality in McCall's life is his mother, Dorothy, who has written two books, about the ranch and her life: *Ranch Under the Rimrock* and *The Copper King's Daughter*. Of his father, Hal, McCall says, "He was a remarkable guy, a less dominant personality than Mother." Hal McCall graduated from Harvard before he came out West.

McCall's paternal grandfather, Samuel McCall, was a three-term governor of Massachusetts and an eminent 20-year Congressman. Before the Crash of 1929, the "Copper King" lost everything he had. His adversaries were not able to take Westernwold, however, because it was in his daughter's name. "Once the Crash happened," says a McCall family member, "it was a matter of, 'What can we sell and who can get work?' The kids worked their way through school."

Hard realities

Perhaps because he was bathed in wealth as a child and the Crash evaporated the wellspring, McCall has never since been financially secure. "There's always been a wolf at the door, that gnawing insecurity," says a newsman who's covered McCall for a long time.

An old friend says, "Tom has never been able to handle money."

The first big break in McCall's life was a speech he made to the Republican Club of Portland in 1949, while he was a radio newscaster. Gov. Douglas McKay was in the audience. McCall says that during the speech a woman, known as the *grande dame* of the Oregon Republican party, leaned over to McKay and said, "There's your man." McKay hired McCall as his assistant.

Today McCall returns to the memory of that "pivotal speech," as he calls it. "I'm sort of living to find out what tomorrow will bring," he says. "Maybe McKay will come after me. In what form I don't know."

Victor Steinbrueck

INTERVIEWED BY DOUG HONIG

Doug Honig is a frequent contributor to the weekly Seattle Sun *and to the* Northwest Passage, *a regional radical journal. He is currently working for KRAB-FM in Seattle under a grant from the Washington Commission for the Humanities. A shorter version of this interview appeared in the May 14, 1980 edition of the* Sun.

Seattle architect, teacher and activist Victor Steinbrueck has published three books of Seattle drawings: Cityscapes 1 *and* 2, *and* Market Sketchbook.

Full-page ads in the Seattle *Times* heralded October 31, 1974 as the 105th anniversary of Seattle's downtown business district. Invitations to celebrate by purchasing party pajamas and Pacesetter dresses were accompanied by boasts of downtown's "Renaissance period — a vigorous transition in architecture, merchandising, and overall updated style."

On page A-14 of that same *Times* — tucked neatly above an article on Nelson Rockefeller — was a letter that began with the clarion call, "Awaken, Seattle! The wreckers are coming!" The letter forecast the impending transformation of First Avenue from a lively melting pot to a chic enclave of trendy business and concluded with the stark warning, "Seattle is burning!"

Its author was architect Victor Steinbrueck, a man ex-mayor Wes Uhlman once called "a very necessary gadfly." Though he has tilted at the edifices of developers and bureaucrats, Steinbrueck is much more than a gadfly. More than any other individual, he was responsible for influencing the popular movement that resulted in preserving Pioneer Square and the Pike Place Market.

Steinbrueck's vision of saving the past comes from no textbook. Born in 1911, Victor Steinbrueck grew up in Auburn and the Georgetown neighborhood of Southwest Seattle and graduated from Franklin High and the University of Washington. He helped design Yesler Terrace, Seattle's first public housing project, before joining the UW faculty in 1946. He won a city-sponsored design contest with his plan for redeveloping Pioneer Square in 1954 and was a leading proponent of establishing an historic preservation commission for the area. A founder of Friends of the Market in the mid-'60s, Steinbrueck was an initiator of the successful 1971 initiative that scuttled city plans for massive redevelopment of the Market. He recently collaborated on the design of Market Park for the Pike Place Urban Renewal Project.

In the following interview, Steinbrueck offers his views of Northwest design and quality of life.

How did your passion for historic preservation develop?
STEINBRUECK: Not in any blinding flash. Architectural history, as I had studied it, came from the East Coast and stopped at Chicago. It was taken for granted that the older stuff out here wasn't important, that it was all blah.

I began to suspect it wasn't true. I found I could learn a lot from old buildings to help in my own work — even obvious stuff such as covering entrances for protection from the rain. So I started having my architecture students do theory projects by examining local neighborhoods in contrast with the typical projects at imaginary sites. Consequently, I became much more interested in common buildings.

Why did you become an activist architect?
STEINBRUECK: I was raised with a fair amount of social consciousness. My father was an active union member, a machinist with the railroads and then the shipyards. My middle name is Eugene — after Eugene Debs. I grew up in a working-class

neighborhood with kids from low-income families as playmates. I always had this feeling that workers were being exploited. I felt that by designing better places to live, I could help people have better lives.

I had been involved in political campaigns and other activities during the Depression, but always separate from my architecture. Then in the late '50s I became concerned about the outrageous locations where highways were being built — through parks and neighborhoods. I felt I had a responsibility to be involved in areas such as this where I had expertise, like a doctor would have responsibility for acting during a plague.

We saw the downtown business interests girding up for the Pike Place Market deal as early as 1959. In fighting against the freeways, the bridges, the loss of buildings, we had always been too late. The plans were prepared in secret, so you wouldn't know what was to be demolished until you saw the wreckers. We felt that if we got involved early, this time we could build an understanding of the urban values that needed preserving.

In politics I've learned to first study an issue carefully and be sure I'm right, then never give up. These urban struggles are an educational process for the public. Often I've felt that we might lose an issue, but that fighting it might help win, or even avoid, the next issue.

Right now, the large-scale projects being done will change the face of downtown. They're produced and approved without public visibility. The developers suddenly present a full-blown model, and there's no chance for modification except through warfare. The environmental impact process helps, but it's done by an advocate of the project and with each project considered separately. Alternatives and overall relationships are not really considered. To me, it's chaos!

So what's your alternative?
STEINBRUECK: Comprehensive planning — a planning process conducted by professionals that democratically involves all parties concerned. The city needs to set priorities for what sorts of activities should happen where. We need an overall process

that coordinates transportation, housing, energy, retail uses, and office development, and that presents the public with choices. I don't mean a rigid plan, but rather a flexible concept of the kind of city we want to have. If, for example, First Avenue is recognized as a necessary part of the city, then we don't allow things that modify it drastically.

Look at transportation. With the number of cars people could be expected to drive to all these new offices being planned, I would guess they won't be able to get off the freeway — the traffic will be too jammed. The lack of planning may force us into one thing that we need, which is mass transit. During this year's ferry strike I noticed thousands of walk-ons — people getting by without automobiles. But I don't think you should wait for disaster to force you to do the right thing.

What do you feel is distinctive about the Northwest?
STEINBRUECK: For one thing, the region has a sense of closeness to wilderness, to primitive space. People have the idea that it's always there, even if you don't utilize it. Mount Rainier is a good symbol — people feel reassured just seeing it.

The open space brings a sense of freedom. A lot of people here have had an independent attitude politically that reflects a feeling of tolerance. People come from a variety of cultural and ethnic backgrounds and seem to get along fairly well. That's partly because we haven't had the economic competition that causes prejudice. There aren't such extremes of wealth and poverty; there's not really bad slums in the Northwest. We have a relatively high percentage of owner-occupied residences, which means people feel less threatened. And if you fear less for your own security, you're less likely to blame other people.

What's this mean for design?
STEINBRUECK: There's less interest in experimenting here. People aren't looking for things special or unique, perhaps because nature is such a tremendous experience in its own right. Residential architects have always been concerned with orienta-

tion toward views and, more recently, have had a growing concern with landscape as part of development.

There's a responsiveness to the climate — the knowledge that there are many overcast days. Architects especially try to take advantage of the sun we do get with larger windows on the south. For a while they were using large expanses of glass. But now they're paying more attention to conservation. There's some interest in solar collectors, though it's still limited. That's obviously the direction in which we have to go.

What kind of architecture do you favor for urban centers?
STEINBRUECK: I'd suggest for our philosophy something Lewis Mumford said: "Plan for lovers and friends." We should design places that are attractive, comfortable, and pleasant for people living and working there. The barefaced concrete, glass, and hard material skins and ordinary shapes of the new buildings downtown in Seattle don't do much for us. They're becoming look-alikes, so that one is going to use blue glass to appear distinctive. They seem designed mainly for maintenance purposes with little regard for the people working there or the passer-by.

I'm not a lover of high-rises — I think they're inhuman. I'd like to see a building limit of six stories, or about sixty feet. It's possible to walk up six floors, and it's a reasonable height you can comprehend; anything above that becomes towering.

A lot of the new projects in Seattle are being done by investors from California and Canada who lack a commitment to the local community. The owners and designers of these edifices don't seem to recognize the real cost of their buildings — their effect on people. Being in them causes a psychological weariness. And the increased density brings civic costs in energy, congestion, and pollution.

How do you see decisions being made about downtown Seattle?
STEINBRUECK: Mostly by large developers such as Weyerhaeuser, Karma, and Daon, who have making money as their

sole goal and while pretending to do some good for the city. They are aided and abetted by City Hall, partly because any development sounds good. Building new buildings means business and financial return for investors and the construction industry, and increased city taxes. But I'm really very concerned about the city's lack of long-range considerations.

A city should be a friendly place to walk around, to explore, to observe, and to mingle with people from all walks of life. You should be able to see necessary human activities, people actually producing things — like in the Market, where you could see real farmers, people cutting meat, maybe baking. The experience of the city as a community is what I'm most concerned about, and I want the architecture and open spaces to accommodate these things.

Of course, there ought to be free public transportation; it's the most economic, efficient way to get around. I'd like to see the city as available to everyone as a village used to be.

How do you now assess your preservation work?
STEINBRUECK: I appreciate that a lot of historic buildings have been saved and that Pioneer Square has acquired a cultural flavor. But I wanted to retain not just buildings, but a place for the people already there and using the area. I especially wanted to keep living accommodations downtown for the native "urban nomads," the Skid Roaders. But single people were always forced out of the area in order to exploit the properties. The single-room-occupancy hotels they lived in simply couldn't bring the same financial return as offices and boutiques which have replaced them.

The Market is still the most colorful people place in the city, but it has been upgraded to where most marginal businesses have lost out, as well as being overrun with crafts merchants. The Mint Dollar Tavern, for example, became the Mint Restaurant with a fancy menu; junk stores were replaced by antique shops. The urban renewal project paid a lot of people to go out of business. The weaker businesses took their relocation payments and just folded up. We need to keep the real character of the Market — as a place related to the lives of local people. A different quality comes from catering to the superficiality of tourism. If it goes too far, the Market will become a completely phony place. It's like fixing up your home for visitors, instead of for your family.

The people who opposed us — downtown developers, banks, property owners, city officials, and bureaucrats — later became in charge of urban renewal. Some have been good, conscientious people, but it reminds me of a South American revolution where the same police stay on to administer the country.

Why fight to save marginal areas?
STEINBRUECK: Because they serve a strata of society that needs to be accommodated. The kind of things that happen on First Avenue, for example, are not available or don't take place anywhere else in the city. Frederick & Nelson and Nordstrom serve a segment of society in their lifestyle. So does First Avenue. It's still the hangout, the living room for urban nomads, Indians, and people working in hard-labor jobs. When the new waterfront projects wipe out First Avenue as their social area, no one knows where they'll go.

It's our economic and social system that produces the people on Skid Road. And if I were down and out, I'd have to go there, too. Society has a responsibility for Skid Road — we can't just sweep those people under the rug.

You've talked mostly of downtown Seattle. What have you seen happening to the city overall?
STEINBRUECK: The weakening of neighborhoods — the loss of a sense of community. As boys, my brother and I explored the city a lot by bicycle and streetcar. I remember Seattle as being much more neighborhood-oriented. Our area of Georgetown, which is now industrial, had an active retail center, with grocery stores and small department stores, and nearby South Park was almost like another town, centered around a school, playfield, and its own shopping center.

I don't recall as much community organization, but there was more sociability. People were on foot more, so they were more likely to say hello when they passed. Neighborhoods had a small town quality; my family was acquainted with a lot of people and knew what was going on here and there. Now community councils are drawing some people together, but mainly in defense against various outrages.

The loss of schools especially hurts. In my own Eastlake neighborhood, I'd like to see our elementary school, which seems to be slated for closure, used for general community activities. It could be kept open with extra rooms rented out to a lawyer and an architect, a printing press, maybe three or four artists, and a real estate firm. It would be educational not only for the children, but also for adults to see different kinds of people than themselves.

What does the future hold?
STEINBRUECK: Regionally, I see a more serious conflict between development and environmental protection — such as the controversy over Weyerhaeuser's plans for the Nisqually Delta or the struggle of people to force I-90 to favor mass transit instead of bringing in more autos. On the one hand, there are economic forces leading to greater pollution and congestion. At the same time, there are more people concerned with doing what's necessary to preserve the environment. People seem to be willing to get together to fight for living qualities they consider important, both in cities and out in the countryside.

Seattle itself is becoming more of a regional center, and development pressures won't be as localized. For instance, I'm afraid the residential area of the Cascade community will be wiped out, though some expensive apartments may move in. I believe neighborhoods such as First Hill, the Central Area, Eastlake, Fremont, and Wallingford will become much higher density and higher cost because of their convenient locations and relatively cheap existing single-family houses.

Seattle is being recognized as one of America's most livable cities, but I have a feeling it used to be a more comfortable place for a person to be with more opportunities for a good life. In the guise of development and economic expansion, we're fast wiping out the human qualities that have made the city livable.

A reporter once asked me during the Market fight, "Do you dream often?" I think you have to. I think things are getting so bad that when all the planned projects become a reality, there will be a reaction. People — and even politicians and developers — will see the need for comprehensive planning. Then we'll have some positive political movement with broader people participation.

Clam Batter

IVAR HAGLUND

Seattle restaurateur Ivar Haglund sells all sorts of seafood, but there is no question that he is best known for clams — Acres of Clams. According to writer Tim Appelo, Ivar has made his bivalves "mythological figures for the Northwest middle class, roughly equivalent to the Shmoos in Li'l Abner."

Go, Savage Clams is the anthem of Ivar's slow-pitch baseball team.

Go, Savage Clams!
Pound 'em into patties!
Go, Savage Clams!
Rip 'em into strips!
Dazzle 'em, and frazzle 'em
And flatten them like kelp!
Go, Savage Clams!
You don't need any help!

James G. Swan

NORMAN H. CLARK

This essay serves as the introduction to the Washington Paperbacks edition of The Northwest Coast, Or, Three Years' Residence in Washington Territory, *by James G. Swan, originally published in 1857. In his published works and his voluminous personal diaries, Swan recorded nearly fifty years of nineteenth-century life on the Olympic Peninsula, providing a rich resource for today's historians and anthropologists. The University of Washington Press published its Washington Paperback edition of* The Northwest Coast *in 1969.*

Norman Clark is on the faculty of Everett Community College. His books include Mill Town, A Social History of Everett, Washington; The Dry Years *and* Deliver Us from Evil, *both about Prohibition; and* Washington, A Bicentennial History.

James Gilchrist Swan was a moral refugee disguised as a businessman when, in 1852, he found shelter and solace in the wilderness of the Northwest Coast. He had chosen a shallow harbor, bound by rock and sand and dark cedar forests, in a season of heavy winds and relentless rains. He was one of perhaps two dozen white Americans then on the Pacific Coast north of the Columbia River. Yet he settled there and built a cedar cabin, happily turning his back on the polite and predictable world of commerce he had left in Boston and on the larger implications of middle-class life in the United States during the days of Daniel Webster and Franklin Pierce. Learned in geography and history, trained in admiralty law, experienced in trade, elegantly schooled in social graces, Swan had nevertheless kicked against the apparently secure and rewarding circumstances of his thirty-four years as a proper New Englander. He had fled from a wife and two children, a prosperous ship-fitting business, and an immeasurable and forever private burden of frustration or remorse or regret. To Swan the West meant the opportunity to shape his life again under circumstances of his own choice. How he did this is one of the subtle dimensions of his narrative of physical and intellectual adventure called *The Northwest Coast*.

Swan escaped under cover of the California gold rush, which, like war, allowed a man to take leave of his obligations and in doing so accept the best wishes of his neighbors and friends. Folded into the anonymous army — more than 10,000 from New England alone — Swan shipped out of Boston in 1849. While the younger men may have talked hysterically of gold and sung "O California! That's the Land for Me," Swan brooded over the richly connotative geography he had learned as a boy at the feet of his seafaring relatives: the Columbia, Destruction Island, Cape Flattery, the Strait of Juan de Fuca, Nootka Sound, Vancouver Island. His interest in gold was at most indifferent, and though he dutifully marched out to the mines that spring, he was back in San Francisco within three months, sick of California and its bonanza society. He took the first ship he could find to the Crown Colony of Vancouver Island, where in an area much larger than that of Massachusetts there were maybe 1,000 white subjects of Great Britain and 30,000 native Indians. He had every intention of staying, but he found himself excluded by the rigid British requirement that immigrants bring servants. Before returning to California, he sailed across the strait to the small sawmill village of Port Townsend, where he thoughtfully filed a claim for free land.

Back in San Francisco, Swan outfitted ships for two years while he again tried to balance the scope of his freedom against the strength of his discretion. During this period he met Charles Russell, then a resident of Shoalwater Bay, just north of the Columbia River, who encouraged Swan to come up the coast. Besides Russell, and under circumstances he never made clear, he also found a strong friendship with the bold and notoriously boozy Clallam Indian named Chetzamakha, better known as the Duke of York. (The Duke's brother was named King George. Swan once described a fishing trip with the Duke of York, whose relatives in the canoe included Jenny Lind, General Gaines, Mrs. Gaines, Queen Victoria, and General Walker.) The Duke was from the Northwest Coast near Port Townsend, and he ignited in Swan a latent but powerful interest in Northwest Indians. With invitations from both the Duke and Russell, Swan now turned his back on California. He eagerly took passage aboard a two-masted squarerigger — and here his book begins — "bound up the Bay for a cargo of piles and spruce-timber," to Shoalwater harbor and the fringes of American influence in a yet unspoiled land.

For an earlier generation of Americans, on the edge of an earlier treasure of natural abundance in the Ohio Valley, it was said that between April and October each year Indian corn made the penniless immigrant into a proud capitalist. With less patience, the gold-rush generation dug up the Sacramento Valley from January to December while a few of the more imaginative adventurers found attractive treasure in the forests of the Northwest Coast. North of the Columbia after 1850 a man could make himself well-to-do in a season by chopping trees with a hand ax, felling them in tide water, then cutting them into logs and firewood to sell to San Francisco. If he had a steam-powered saw — and Swan noted sawdust thirty miles out to sea from the mouth of the Columbia — he could make himself wealthy. If he wanted to farm, he could ship to the fantastic prices in San Francisco for potatoes, butter, or wheat. California would buy almost anything that was for sale, and along the Northwest Coast shrewd men were looking for almost anything.

The men Swan met there were all newcomers to the region, free spirits in no way cramped by the history or traditions of the missionary-ridden society of pioneer farmers that had since 1834 nourished American loyalties in the Willamette Valley of Oregon. Oregon was to them irrelevant. They would have been appalled by the thought of enduring the rigors of the Oregon

Trail, the Oregon Temperance Society, or the Methodist Church. They had never been to Oregon City, nor did they know the famous Jessie Applegate, leader of wagon trains and pioneers, or General Joseph Lane, former governor of Oregon Territory and in 1852 their own delegate to Congress. Nor did they care. They had come not to farm but to cut gold out of the sea and the forest, to plunder timber from lands they did not own, to pack salmon and shellfish from the seemingly endless rivers and bays, or simply to sell whiskey to the Indians.

But their ambitions were not always consistent, and there was relief here from the California frenzy. The oysters of Shoalwater Bay, just as the Indian corn of the Ohio Valley, could make more than a few of the immigrants into incorrigible slobs. The "oyster boys" of Swan's retreat were taking the brightest nuggets from the top of a fabulous abundance, and they could do it with a minimum of labor. Swan's host, Charles Russell, had Indians and their slaves raking up piles of shellfish and loading them aboard the California schooners. This was capitalism in the grand manner: he and Swan sitting in the comfort of a rough cabin before the warmth of a bottle and a blazing fire, savoring the depth of their own insights while the Indians labored to make them rich.

But as a way of life, oyster picking was so directly bound to the uncertainties of wind and tide that the man accepting them could not be impatient. What he made in one raking he might lose with the next. The Indians would work only spasmodically and according to their own inclinations, not those of the San Francisco market. Given these conditions, and the adversity of weather and communications, grand plans were the essence of folly.

Yet the affluence was there for the daily taking — fish, clams, oysters, crabs, fowl, game — and one could live very well. And there was also the genial fellowship that Swan found among "generous and noble-hearted men." The drunks and the Indians had found a more or less satisfactory cultural mutuality of some advantage to both. In this wet and miserable forest — which could sometimes be gloriously fresh and crisp in green woods, brown sand, white waves and blue sea — there was a sense of community. In its relationship to American values and energies in the 1850s, it was not an alien community, but it was an alienated one, and Swan eagerly became a part of it. For a brief moment before the Civil War, the railroads, the machines and the factories, Shoalwater Bay sheltered a leisurely society of boozy white loafers and boozy but friendly Indians who lived untroubled by the currents of progress and naturally protected from any windy convictions about the perfectibility of man.

Swan's achievement in this community was that he soon had more influence among the Indians than any other American. This seems to have come almost naturally to him — from his real interest in the Indians and his way of letting them know he was interested, from his ability to accept them as individuals of importance and integrity. He studied their languages and soon spoke them fluently. He ate their food, walked the beaches with them, learned to feel secure when rolled up in a blanket in an Indian lodge. He approached the deeply human problem of cross-cultural communication with humility and intelligence, and the rapport he found brought him a deeply personal fulfillment. This is not to say that Swan went native, for he was much too thoroughly New England and Anglo-Saxon to suspend his basic assumptions about nature and man. But for an American in the 1850s, even for one with serious intellectual and artistic needs, Swan had a degree of tolerance, of curiosity, of broad-mindedness, and of sensitivity that was indeed remarkable. It may have been the truest measure of his alienation from his own society.

Because he could appreciate the difference of Indian cultural values without denying their integrity for Indians, Swan could feel the terrible threat that white Americans raised to Indian culture with their guns and machines, their whiskey, theft, competition, and unequal justice. He could see enough of himself in the Indians to know that they should regard most Americans as casual vanguards of a foreign horde that would force upon them a foreign language, unintelligible customs, and a meaningless religion, and in doing so destroy their identity as Indians. In his moments of solemn clarity — and this is his greatest achievement for readers today — he could see himself as both observer of and participant in a barbaric invasion.

The Indians of the Northwest Coast that Swan came to know were then passing between the twilight of their tranquility and the night of their most desperate affliction. The hour was late: small-pox, measles, and syphilis had already swept grimly over a be-wildered people. Since their first contact with Europeans in the eighteenth century, the mortality among some groups was as high as 90 percent. And thereafter the demoralized remnants of a strong and vigorous society fell easily to the debauchery of drunkenness and to the social confusion of new wealth as they took rum, metal, and blankets from the maritime fur traders.

As early as 1805 the Chinook Indians at the mouth of the Co-lumbia River were, as Lewis and Clark found them, decorated with foreign tattoos and beads, dressed in manufactured blankets and sailors' clothes, addicted to whoredom and theft, and suffering from "Venerious and pustelus disorders."[1] But they were still a "mild and inoffensive"[2] people with great reserves of character and stability. They took the fevers in the 1830s, and twenty years later Swan saw them as "a miserable, whiskey-drinking set of vagabonds," a people whose "race is nearly run." At the time of Lewis and Clark they had numbered maybe 5,000. Swan counted fewer than 100.

The natives Swan lived with north of the river had seen fewer whites and fewer calamities. When he knew them in the 1850s, the diseases were among them, but they could still present clear features of an affluent and sophisticated culture. They were rich, first of all, in salmon and cedar. And having an abundance of the necessities of life, they enriched themselves in life's satisfactions. In their fishing, hunting, and gathering, they drew a deep emo-tional security from mutual participation. In the wide circles of

1. Clark, in Bernard DeVoto, ed., *The Journals of Lewis and Clark* (1953).
2. Lewis, in his *Lewis and Clark Expedition*, ed. Archibald Hanna (1961).

their extended-family relationships, as Swan observed, they cared for their old people with sympathy and dignity, and they honored their children with affection and respect.

They were rich also in leisure and aesthetic sensibility. The artistry of the song and dance Swan recorded touched every individual. Almost every aspect of their lives, in fact, was invested with aesthetic significance. The coming of salmon in the spring inspired an elaborate and delicate ritual, and the fish clubs used daily by the men could be refined into a reflection of grace and pleasure. The baby's cradle sketched by Swan shows a natural integration of utility and beauty.

They were rich, furthermore, in the harmony of their interpersonal relationships. A coastal village might have several families whose personal wealth and consequent social status brought them high esteem. These rich people, whom Swan saw as "chiefs," might advise or encourage others to do their will, but seldom did they have the power or authority to coerce individuals or to commit the group collectively to any course of action. Law and order was a matter of praise or ridicule from influential individuals like Swan's friend Old Toke. Violence was seldom if ever a part of social discipline. This tranquility was in striking contrast to the snarling and brawling, whipping and hanging among the whites of Swan's society from whom the Indians were even then learning.

Even so, the Indians north of the Columbia had for years lived peacefully with the employees of Hudson's Bay Company, the powerful British monopoly whose Columbia Department was so intelligently administered. In the 1820s the company had built Fort Vancouver, and from this cedar castle by the wide river it brought sanity and stability to an entire region. Through its rocklike policies of fairness for the natives, discipline for the whites, an end to cutthroat competition in the fur trade, prohibition of liquor, and the conservation of fur resources, the company became an institutional force for law and order and church and state. Under the leadership of the wise and imperious Dr. John McLoughlin — a giant of a man with flowing white hair and a gold-headed cane — the company came not to wreck the native culture but to understand it. Hudson's Bay Company men worked with the Indians, mingled freely with them, gained their confidence by learning how to appeal to their sense of private property and by teaching them to be of service both to themselves and to London. Gentlemen and men of the marching brigades took Indian wives and raised families. As a bridge between two very different cultures, the Hudson's Bay Company was perhaps the most humane and effective ever conceived by Europeans for North America. It was by far superior to either slavery or war.

It is a tragedy of American history that American values in the 1840s and 1850s were so consistent with slavery and war. Brutally racist and piously arrogant, the United States brought war to Mexico in 1846 so that Americans could seize the promised land of California. And threatening this same belligerence — with wild talk of 54–40 or Fight or of taking all of Canada — James Polk's government forced the British into the Oregon Treaty that same year and into withdrawing to lands beyond the Strait of Juan de Fuca. Though the treaty allowed Hudson's Bay Company to retain certain rights to its properties, the blatant outlawry of American squatters was making the company's position untenable by the time Swan arrived in 1849. For the Indians, the Oregon Treaty meant the collapse of a system that had sustained them with honor for a generation, and it meant the coming of men who held the system and the Indians themselves in ugly contempt. Americans validated their own greed with land laws which provided invaders like Swan with free land before they ever thought of Indian treaties. Most Americans who came with Swan regarded the Indians quite simply as a public menace, free targets for any treachery or for wanton murder. Even before 1850 the United States Government of Oregon Territory had brought war to the Rogues and to the Cayuse and driven both groups relentlessly toward extermination.

A terrible insight into their future could not long escape the others. If they protested sometimes with violence, it was not without terrifying cause. During the "wars" of the 1850s in the new governmental division of Washington Territory, Americans ruthlessly crushed these protests with search-and-destroy missions that were consistent with the treatment that barbarians have usually accorded civilized populations: rape, concentration camps, hostages, arbitrary and summary execution, and outright murder. Thus it was that Colonel George Wright, in 1858 having destroyed the Indians' winter supply of food, ordered the young Yakima leader Qualchin to appear before him and warned that refusal would mean death for hostages, among whom was the leader's aged father. Wright reported that "Qualchin came to me at 9 o'clock and at 9¼ a.m. he was hung." And thus it was that Charles Grainger, a simpleminded deputy sheriff, was ordered the same year to a lonely prairie east of Fort Steilacoom to hang Leschi, the respected leader of Puget Sound Indians, because the 36 rapacious men of the Territorial Legislature wanted to rob these Indians of their finest intelligence and teach them more terror. Even the United States Army and the same Colonel Wright refused to recognize that the government had any legitimate grievance against so noble a man. Leschi in his last words said that he would not be the first man to lose his life on false evidence. If he was dying for his people, he said, he was "willing to die. Christ died for others." Grainger later told a friend that "I felt that I was executing an innocent man."

It was during the rush of this violence that Swan was preparing his book, and one must note that his explanations of "war" in the 1850s are not distinguished by their moral authority. He wanted, on the one hand, to have his readers see the Indians as he had come to know them. He wanted to say why he felt a peaceful and productive coexistence between the two races was possible. For the Indians to survive, he believed, they must be free to nurture their own cultural identity and free to resist the cultural tyranny of white Americans.

He knew that the system of forcing the Indians to live on reservations was not conceived in this belief. He knew too of trickery, deceit, and murder, for even his friend the Duke of York was taken hostage. Swan wanted to make it clear that he would be no apologist for American outrages.

Yet at the same time he was serving as secretary to Isaac Stevens, the delegate to Congress and former governor of Washington Territory who had designed the treaties, imposed them upon the Indians, and first called for war. Swan had been an interpreter for Stevens and apparently held him in high regard. Part of Swan's assignment, in fact, was to help Stevens win Congressional approval for the treaties. The result, in Chapter XX of *The Northwest Coast*, is a combination of significant anthropological insight with an absurdly ethnocentric polemic in which Swan seemed to blame Hudson's Bay Company and the American army leaders more than he blamed American farmers, lumber pirates, and Governor Stevens.

Clearly, Swan never saw himself as a social critic. He did, however, want a reputation as an ethnologist, but he never attained any generous measure of it from a society not yet awakened to social science. Whatever fame or personal glory Swan knew — and this was never enough to keep him in security or confidence — was almost entirely local fame as a local colorist, a man who had written a book about vivid episodes of the pioneer past.

Swan could spin a good story. His opening sentence of the *Northwest Coast* has a crisp Victorian ring that promises excitement, mystery, or humor, and the chapters that follow are built on sturdy paragraphs, occasionally bright with the flash of a perfect metaphor. His readers have felt quickly at home in the quiet tide pools of Shoalwater society. Swan's careful descriptions have helped readers to imagine the Indians and to picture the whites, like Big Charley, the good-natured, lazy constable, who, "like some stray spar or loose

kelp, has been washed up into the Bay without exactly knowing when, where, or how.'' Or Champ, the Justice of the
Peace, who ''although he could sign his name, could not see to
read very well, having smashed his spectacles on a frolic.''
And Swan could sometimes reach beyond local color to the
deep and even prophetic sadness of men like Old Toke, the
lonely Indian who had known high status and prestige but
whom whiskey had reduced to contempt and ridicule.

Swan could also focus on the exuberant absurdities of frontier life. In the infinity of space and natural abundance,
dozens of Americans creep out of the woods to seek shelter
from a storm and gather themselves in an eight-by-ten house
to suffer discomforts considerably more profuse than those
of the wind and rain without. A fantastic skipper of a San
Francisco schooner, to whom people entrust their lives and
fortunes, makes trip after trip with a lordly vanity that causes
him to wear green goggles which render him practically blind.
In the story of the frightful storm that brought chaos and
destruction to Swan's house and properties, there is enough
humor in pure misery to move the reader toward laughter as
well as pain.

Besides pathos and absurdity, Swan sometimes fixed un-
knowingly upon the apocalyptic. There is a scene in which the
enflamed oyster boys roared to the climax of a Fourth of July
by setting afire an entire forest that burned until the winter
rains came — a scene of such thoughtless folly and impulsive
madness that it could stand as a profoundly allegorical comment on the history of the American West.

Swan's most profound comment, however, lies in the im-
balance of serious and foolish matters that marked his life
after he left Shoalwater Bay. He went east again, to see to the
publication of his book and to serve Isaac Stevens for two
years in Washington, D.C. Then on Stevens' advice he returned to the Olympic Peninsula and settled near his land
claim at Port Townsend, where he waited for the railroads to
come and convert his land into his belated bonanza.

It was hard waiting. He did pieces for newspapers of Boston and San Francisco (their "correspondent in Washington Territory") and began a law practice, which in Port Townsend was more a hobby than a profession. The diaries he kept during these years are voluminous records of his day-to-day events and observations, even temperatures and tides, all of them neat, methodical, and literate. One wonders if he wrote all this with any conviction that his life in a muddy sawmill village glowed with a message or a vision that he would somehow, someday, cast into words and books. In these thousands of pages there is no hint that he did. Nor is there any implicit thrust or spirit, any insights, questions, or indignations. They are not the work of a dedicated artist or scholar or even of a self-consciously literary man.

The waiting aroused other passions. In 1864 Swan stood for election to the territorial legislature, but he was decisively defeated. Even then his surest instincts were to refine his sensitivities to Indian culture and do with this what he could. He spent four years with the Makah Indians at Neah Bay, learning their language, observing their customs, and helping these people do a thousand things, from administering medicines to building houses and discouraging drunken mayhem. In 1868 he produced a small volume of observation, scholarship, and drawings about the Makahs for the Smithsonian Institution. One can say of this book, *The Indians of Cape Flattery*, that the government got its money's worth, whatever it paid for it. The work was probably as perceptive as any work being done in anthropology by any American at that time. If it is disappointing today, it is because the study lacks discipline and because Swan always choked on matters of interpersonal relationships. But at that time anthropology was not a discipline and no American scholar was articulate about such matters. Had Swan been able to conceptualize a science and practice it as we know it a century later, we would indeed regard him as a very great man, just as we would if he had cried out against the wars and treaties a full generation before the Indian Rights Association or Helen Hunt Jackson's *A Century of Dishonor.*

But Swan was not then seeking greatness. He wrote, he waited. He tried to do what as a younger man he had said was impossible — to make whites of the Indians by organizing and teaching school at Neah Bay. This was, the diary recorded, "the most unsatisfactory thing I ever tried." He quit it and spent the rest of his long life in Port Townsend, living precariously from his gift for a felicitous phrase and his sure touch for the sinecure: customs agent, secretary to the Puget Sound Pilots' Commission, "teacher and dispenser of medicine" for the Indians, correspondent for the Smithsonian, occasional counselor in admiralty law, surveyor of boats, ticket agent for a steamship company, notary public, probate judge, and, in his very old age — it sounds like a cruel joke — "Counsel for Hawaii at Port Townsend." In all, he lived from hand to mouth, using his land claim as an annuity by selling small pieces, and performing odd jobs of simple literacy in a society where simple literacy was in demand. In the 1870s he received a small grant to do a study for the Smithsonian. *The Haidah Indians of Queen Charlotte's Island, British Columbia* was the last and most superficial of his books.

He was then deeply involved in elaborate fantasies inspired by the transcontinental railroads, for he really believed that Port Townsend was the natural terminal for the Northern Pacific, that the railroad would make Port Townsend into a metropolis, the gateway to the Orient, the storehouse for the riches of the Pacific Northwest. Swan had even ingratiated himself with the directors of that railroad, having since 1868 offered them detailed, literate, and warmly impractical advice about their best interest on Puget Sound and the Northwest Coast. These directors apparently encouraged him to believe that his advice was being taken seriously. He once accompanied a party of railroad capitalists and bankers on a trip down sound aboard the steamer *Cyrus Walker* and soberly read for them his paper entitled "The Amoor River: The Countries Drained By The Amoor River And

Its Tributaries And The Imminent Trade Now Lying Dormant In Siberia, Mongolia, Manchooria, Northern China, Korea, And Japan Which Will Be Brought Into Active Life And Diverted To The American Shore Of The North Pacific Ocean By The Great Continental Railroads Which Will Have The Outlet Of Their Commerce Through The Straits Of Fuca To The Great Ocean Of The West.''

In the late 1870s Swan was presenting himself as an agent of the Northern Pacific, which he may in some minor way have been, though there is no evidence that he ever enjoyed any of the railroad's prosperity. During these years Judge Swan became a monument of sorts in the sawmill town and in the territory. He knew the charity of his friends, who in turn knew Swan as an increasingly alcoholic ''character'' — a handsome, white-haired and neatly bearded gentleman in his sixties, the unofficial intellectual who, it was rumored, would someday write a great history of Washington Territory. The next generation remembered him as a ''picturesque figure'' who took no part in the commercial life of the city but who was always ready to accept a drink or a dinner, ready to suffer the deliberations of the local pioneer clubs and moral reform societies, to march in a parade, or to deliver a speech on any public occasion.

Toward the end of that decade the wealthy Hubert Howe Bancroft came north from San Francisco to gather raw materials for the books of western history that made him famous. He stopped in Port Townsend to see ''Judge James G. Swan, ethnologist, artist, author . . .'' Bancroft was distressed to find so distinguished a gentleman, scholar, and pioneer-adventurer living behind a translucent alcoholic curtain. Swan was so drunk that day that he refused to see Bancroft until he could sober up, and Bancroft waited, lamenting for the ''poor fellow'' whom ''demon Drink had long held . . . in his terrible toils.'' At length, however, Swan was his gracious best, and he happily unloaded upon the historian thirty years' notes and artifacts and long conversations about his early experiences. Bancroft footnoted this generosity with his observation that Judge Swan had "occupied many public places of more honor than profit."

Swan must have been utterly demoralized by 1887 when it was clear that Tacoma, and not Port Townsend, would get the Northern Pacific. The dream of two decades was gone, and he was suddenly an old man. Then, most cruelly, the remaining value of his land was washed away by the depression that hit in 1893. Port Townsend thereafter became a hollow shell of a community. Some of its brick buildings, built for the coming of the railroads, have gone without tenants ever since. Swan stayed on. At the age of 75, he had no place to go and no desire to find one. He stayed in a smoky one-room house, living like the Indians, cooking for himself, sinking into total obscurity — a patriarch in a ghost town, a master of poverty, a sometime poet of the frontier forgotten on the edge of an industrial world.

At his death in 1900 at the age of 82, Swan had nothing but a room full of grease-covered books, his meticulous diaries, and a few minor debts. His life had been a confusion of goals, sensitivities, and values, a drama of quiet desperation played out in a dark and deep wilderness that was the Northwest Coast. In his thirties he had broken like a prisoner from the chains of middle-class securities, free to find his own truth in his own way. In his forties he had abandoned his experiment in freedom among the oyster pickers; for, like Henry Thoreau, he had other lives to lead. In his fifties he had turned away from serious scholarship and from his twenty-years' investment in rapport with the Indians. In his sixties he tried to make money; but in his seventies he gave this up also, and along with it, perhaps, any hope for recognition, or dignity, or even fellowship. His joys were his energy, curiosity, and intellectuality that would have been admirable in any man, especially one so friendly and generous. Whatever his anxieties, his spiritual wounds or griefs, he did not commit them to record. His great misfortune was to live in a society so merciless in its judgment of those whose broad and multipurposed talents led them in many directions and excluded them from the rewards of single-minded men.

In this century Swan's Shoalwater Bay has been known as Willapa Bay. Its great forests are gone, but its shallow water has kept it from becoming the commercial port that Swan once imagined. It is still a quiet region, a delight to the eye, not everywhere clattering with people and machines. Opening westward to the Pacific, the land can still suggest the deeply sensuous experiences that James Swan so happily embraced. The Shoalwater Indian Reservation rims the north shore, and Tokeland, named after Old Toke, is as wind-swept and drunken-gray in the rain and as magnificently blue and green and salty pure in the sunshine as Swan described it. North of the bay and beyond Gray's Harbor there are wilderness strips of beach protected by the Olympic National Park that remain just as Swan knew them, with miles of sand, a million tide pools in the rocks, storm-shaped headlands, impenetrable forests, and the soft silence of woods and sea.

Swan's Diaries

JAMES G. SWAN

Swan was in his early sixties, in the middle of his fifty years of living on the Northwest coast, when he made these diary entries. Each day's recounting began with a synopsis of the weather, including three temperature readings, wind velocities, and a description of the cloud cover. Swan also included a log of the ships that entered and left the harbor at Neah Bay and a list of his inspections as customs officer.

Some punctuation has been added to avoid confusion, but Swan's spellings of people's names and place names have been retained. The diaries, along with correspondence and other material, are in the archives of the Suzzallo Library at the University of Washington.

Neeah Bay
Wednesday, July 23, 1879

. . . At 8 a.m. there was a fine fog bow not colored like a rainbow but pure white. This was at the head of the bay and the arc of the bow extended from Koilta [?] point to Klesedetsose. It lasted half an hour or more and looked very similar in brightness to lunar halo. 2 p.m. fine clear weather.

. . . Chadelth, Mary Ann's brother brought me a stone with a fossil in it.

I noticed several marigold blossoms which had gone to seed have again sprouted and blossomed in the old seed capsule. I counted one which had 14 in full bloom. This is occasioned by the wet weather we have had all the spring and summer.

Examined 2 canoes from Vancouver Island with fish and mats.

Neeah Bay
Thursday, July 24, 1879

. . . Dr. Power took my little pickaxe to Mr. Wier [?] this morning to have a new handle put in and on his return this evening brought me a bottle of cough mixture, as my cold and cough is quite troublesome.

Martha, Minnie, Hattie and Ginger came this afternoon and procured flowers to decorate themseles. They preferred the large marigolds.

This evening three Clyoquot Indians came to see the picture of Maquilla and Callicum in Mears book. Their names are Ya áetin or Johnny, Mamákwi or Joe, and Klaklak or Pat. The last named is a savage looking chap. They have come to invite the Makahs to a potlatch. They say there is no sickness at Clyoquot . . . .

Neeah Bay
Friday, July 25, 1879

. . . Finished letter to Cleopas B. Johnson, Medford, Mass. and then commenced writing an address for the Port Townsend Emigrant Aid Society.

. . . This evening some of the hands on board the *Blakely* played several tunes on some brass instruments. I thought the music sounded pretty well but I asked Martha how she liked it and she said it sounded like crows and blue jays and was not as nice music as Mr. Willoughby makes on the organ . . . .

Neeah Bay
Saturday, July 26, 1879

. . . The Indians started very early this morning for Clyoquot to attend a potlatch. Jimmy went in his canoe with a big crowd.

Peter was the last off owing to his having to come up to the agency to sign some papers. He says they will be about a week. Asked him to get me a bark blanket and a Clyoquot hat.

This morning I cut some thyme to dry for herb stuffing. It was in full bloom and very nice.

Went to Neeah and mailed a package containing 6 table mats directed to Cleopas B. Johnson, Medford, Mass. Paid postage on same. 10¢ . . . .

Neeah Bay
Monday, July 28, 1879

. . . Pleasant morning and pleasant day.

Measured a stalk of white foxglove in my flower bed, and found it 7 feet 8 inches high.

. . . The Indians have commenced catching salmon and bringing them in for sale. Yesterday Albert brought some 25 "Sooit" to Capt. Willoughby, and today he had his tank cleaned out and salted them.

Neeah Bay
Tuesday, July 29, 1879

. . . Carried my wash clothes to Annie Bolin this PM as I intend going to Port Townsend as soon as possible.

Caught 3 mice in traps and gave them to little Janji and Minnie and Emma Demm [?]. They were highly pleased and carried them off to show to Mary Ann.

Port Townsend
Friday, August 1, 1879

. . . Received my salary for July — $101.10.

Port Townsend
Tuesday, August 5, 1879

. . . Paid Peterson for cleaning and repairing clothes — $3.50 and Maj. Van Bokkelen in acct. for rent — $20.00

Bought at Jay's China Store a plate cup and saucer — $3.00, postage and box — $ .60, directed box to Ellen M. Swan and sent by mail.

Paid CC Bartlett bill in full to date — $58.98.

Quilleute
Tuesday, August 19, 1879

. . . Noticed an old woman in Howealth's lodge who was preparing the fibre from nettle stalks. The leaves and branches are first stripped off and the stalk partially dried over the fire, then each stalk is split open with a sharpened bone or piece of deer horn and the woody part broke with the fingers and peeled off from the fibre which is the outside skin or bark of the nettle. It is a tedious and slow way of preparing the fibre and I observed that little is now used for twine as they find that twine prepared by white men is cheaper and preferable. I think if the nettle could be rotted like hemp, that the fibre could be quite easily prepared and the quantity growing wild every where about the [illegible] yield an abundant supply.

Neeah Bay
Tuesday, December 25, 1879

Christmas (Rainy day)

3 inches of snow fell yesterday at 9 p.m. Soon after midnight drizzly misty rain and this morning gentle rain which increased and continued falling heavily all day. Weather thick, bay smooth, no surf.

Temperature milder. 7 a.m. — 34. 10 a.m. — 44.

Took our breakfast this morning in the new dining room which is very comfortable and pleasant. I did not eat much as I had not quite recovered my attack of last evening. Decorated my office with ferns and evergreens and made a wreath of the colored moss which Fanny David dyed for me. It looks very pretty.

This forenoon Fanny David and another girl came up and made me a visit of two hours duration. After they had gone Ellen and Minnehaha came and I treated them to boiled eggs.

We had a very nice dinner today. Roast Turkey, Roast Goose, cranberry sauce, onions, turnips, potatoes, Plum pudding, mince pie and cake.

Gone West

IVAN DOIG

This is an excerpt from Winter Brothers: A Season at the Edge of America. *The book uses James Swan's diaries and Ivan Doig's more personal reflections on his own westward progress to examine the nature of the Northwest and the westering impulse. Ivan Doig's first book,* This House of Sky, *recalled the formation of "a western mind" during the author's childhood in his native Montana. Doig now lives north of Seattle and is at work on his first novel.*

Sawed wood — firewood — decides my site when I am here inside the cabin. I settle at the kitchen table, close by the cookstove which must be fed each hour or so. (Howard has told me he will harvest his own firewood when summer comes, from the stand of alder woven within the mullioned window. A neighbor who owns a team of workhorses will skid the downed trees in for sawing. I wish the harnessed horses were there now, the leather sounds of their working heft coming down the mountainside. Instead, if anything is out there, it will be either Solo on reconnaissance to see whether I have mended my anti-dog ways, or the slowly gliding deer.) Today out of the mound of mail which has been building on my desk since Swan's diaries moved into my days I finally have winnowed the letter from Mark, in his faculty office in Illinois — we may be the last two American friends who write regularly and at such length to one another — and the quote which he found during his research on mid-nineteenth-century frontier missionaries. The Reverend John Summers, reporting from Benton County, Iowa, in July of 1852:

"A young man recently left for California, who for two years has been very anxious to go, but during his minority had been restrained by the influence and authority of his parents. They offered, for the sake of diverting him from his purpose, to furnish him the means to travel and visit the Eastern cities. He derided the idea. He would not turn his hand over to see all that could be seen in the East, but he must go to the Utopia of the New World; and he has gone."

Gone west and cared not so much as a flip of his hand to know any of that lesser land behind him. In all but flesh, that young Iowan was my grandfather, my great-uncles, my father and his five brothers, me. After my Doig grandparents sailed from Scotland and crossed America to a high forest-tucked valley of the Rocky Mountains nobody of the family for two generations ever went to the Atlantic again. When I journeyed off to college I was spoken of as being "back east in Illinois." My father adventured to Chicago once on a cattle train and twice to visit me. My mother, after her parents moved from Wisconsin to the Rockies when she was half a year old, never returned beyond the middle of Montana.

This westernness in my family, then, has been extreme as we could manage to make it. We lived our first seventy years as Americans on slopes of the Rockies as naturally, single-mindedly, as kulaks on the Russian steppes. (Nights when I have been at my desk reading Swan's pages I have noticed that my square-bearded face reflected in the desk-end window could be a photographic plate of any of those museful old Scotsmen who transplanted our family name to the western mountains of America. If we have the face we deserve at forty — or thirty-nine and some months, as I am now — evidently I am earning my way backwards to my homesteading grandfather.) My own not very many years eastward, which is to say in the middle of the Mid-west, amounted to a kind of instructive geographic error. (Instructive, literally: Montana as evaluated at Northwestern University in Evanston, 1957: "youse guys," confides my new college friend from The Bronx, "youse guys from Mwawntana twalk funny.") The journalism jobs in the flat-horizoned midland turned my ambition in on itself, impelled me to work the salaried tasks for more than they were worth and to sluice the accumulating overflow of ideas into pages of my own choice. Also, happiest result of my brief misguess of geography (chiding from a friend who had stepped back and forth among writing jobs: "It doesn't matter any more where you live in this country." It matters.), I met Carol there, already edging west on her own, and when the two of us turned together, away from editorial careers and ahead to independence, we stepped a fourth of the continent farther than any of my family had done. Puget Sound's salt water begins six hundred yards from our valley-held house close by Seattle.

And so with Swan, I judge. When the reverend wrote those opining words Swan of Boston already had been on the Pacific shore for two years and was about to head onward to Shoalwater Bay and ultimately the Strait and Cape Flattery. Finding the place to invest his life meant, as it has to me, finding a west. (Roulette of geography, of course, that the American frontier stretched from the Atlantic toward the Pacific instead of the other way around. Erase *Santa Maria* and *Mayflower*, ink in Chinese junks anchoring at San Francisco Bay and Puget Sound four hundred years ago, re-read our history with its basis in Confucianism, its exploit of transcontinental railroads laid across the eastern wilderness by quaint coolie labor from London and Paris, its West Coast mandarins — the real item — aloofly setting cultural style for the country.) What Swan and his forty-year wordstream will have told me by the end of this winter, this excursion back where I have never been, I can't yet know. But already I have the sense from his sentences and mine that there are and always have been many wests, personal as well as geographical. (Even what I have been calling the Pacific Northwest is multiple. A basic division begins at the Columbia River; south of it, in Oregon, they have been the sounder citizens, we in Washington the sharper strivers. Transport fifty from each state as a colony on Mars and by nightfall the Oregonians will put up a school and a city hall, the Washingtonians will establish a bank and a union.) Swan on the Strait has been living in two distinct ones, Neah Bay and Port Townsend (and sampled two others earlier, San Francisco and Shoalwater Bay) and neither of them is the same as my own wests, Montana of a quarter-century ago and Puget Sound of today. Yet Swan's wests come recognizable to me, are places which still have clear overtones of my own places, stand alike with mine in being distinctly unlike the rest of the national geography. Perhaps that is what the many wests are, common in their stubborn separatenesses: each west a kind of cabin, insistent that it is no other sort of dwelling whatsoever.

Wild Salmon

BRUCE BROWN

This is a chapter from a book in progress on the wild salmon of the Olympic Peninsula. Bruce Brown is a former reporter for the Seattle Times, *the Seattle* Post-Intelligencer *and* Argus Magazine. *He lives in Sumas, Washington.*

I was watching hundreds of pink salmon scatter the last, lurid light of evening across the Graywolf River when I heard the sound again. It was a faint, quavering cry, and as it rose and fell above the roar of the river, it was impossible to tell if it came from one throat, or one thousand. Harsh and somehow urgent, it seemed to be echoing from the heart of the mountains.

The Graywolf, which drains the high valley between Blue Mountain and the Graywolf Pinnacles east of Port Angeles, is noted for its peculiar auditory mirages. Solitary travelers seem particularly susceptible to the "river voices," but groups of people and even animals have heard them as well: I once saw a deer browsing on the bench above Divide Creek prick its ears and listen intently to these same faraway sounds.

Fifty years ago this steep valley rang with the howling of the wolves that gave the river its name. The now extinct Olympic Peninsula timber wolves favored the Graywolf above all others, and made their last stand against the government-paid killers in its upper reaches. Straining to hear faint sounds in the deepening dusk, I could imagine the greenish-orange embers in their eyes a little too well, and hunkered down into my big, smoky mackinaw.

The sun had left the valley floor at 3 p.m., and now, six hours later, my wait was nearly over. In front of my camp lay what is probably the single richest spawning grounds on the Olympic Peninsula for pink salmon, *Oncorhynchus gorbuscha*. As soon as it was dark, I planned to wade the river and observe the fishes' nocturnal cavortings. I had memorized the river carefully, for although I was carrying a flashlight, stealth demanded that I travel in complete darkness.

It was late August, and the Graywolf summer pink run was swelling to the first of its three climactic waves. I had been following these pinks (considered very choice because they come into the river earlier than any other pink run on the peninsula) since before dawn, when I spotted a six-pound male between two boulders the color of rotten ice. He had a high, knife-edged hump flying like a burgundy banner above the water, hooked snout and rainbow across his tail that caught fire as the sun cleared the opposite ridge, charging the river with color and revealing thousands of diaphanous dew-covered cobwebs on the branches of the trees.

Further on, I found several dozen pairs of pinks fighting their way up a riffle into a narrow crack of cloudless sky. Here the flat-sided males were less adept than their sleek, black-lipped consorts. Several times I saw males washed down with the current when females passed easily into the small patch of smooth water above. With a fall of 3,000 feet in seventeen miles, the Graywolf is one of the swiftest rivers in the west, dancing white and foaming between the mountains, and always moving down. Because it is not glacial like the Dungeness (which it joins in the foothills of the Olympics), the Graywolf is so clear in late summer that one can actually see the air ripped into it wherever it surges over rock or log.

Pinks will pick out isolated spawning pockets when necessary, but their tribal nature encourages them to congregate on the river's few large spawning grounds. When I arrived at my present camp, I found the river alive with wild humpy males chasing each other in wide gyres across the smooth, 150-yard-long glide where the river flowed at a depth of two feet over a beautifully graveled bed. Redds extended in bunches from the edge of the lower fall-away up to the pool at the base of the riffle above. One popular female with a white belly and broad black stripe down her side sent her half dozen suitors into a tizzy every time she rolled on her side to excavate the redd. As each puff of silt drifted away on the current, one or more males raced downstream several hundred feet, spun around like tail-skidding dirt track speedsters, and dashed back.

Another ripe dame with pink crescents on her gills and an iridescent green head was run over by one of her own suitors in the confused jostling around the redd. She and the other females seemed willing to indulge the most extreme behavior by the males, but let one of their own sex become involved in the act and the situation changed dramatically. When one female dug too close to the redd of another, which seemed to be happening everywhere simultaneously, the proprietress would rocket after the offender. Their chases were much faster and more gracefully executed than those of the males, and when they caught each other they tore savagely at each other's fins and other exposed parts. Like the males, however, they were seldom able to discourage their challengers, with the result that the same fish would repeat the game of Advance, Chase and Retreat for days until one of them no longer had enough life left to continue.

On the heart of the glide a mass of salmon was wheeling in an endless circuit, drifting sideways to expose their broad sides when hostile, and gliding past each other like fingers into a glove when not. Viewed from the shore, the pinks appeared as a shifting lavender stain on the sunny river bottom. There were probably 100 redds on the glide, and several times that many fish. Upriver, another group of fish had holed up in the pool, where they were leaping at lazy intervals. Most of these fish (which I took to be part of the second wave) were not yet ripe, but among them were also some consumed and seemingly spastic fish bumping along the shoreline, and two white carcasses which glowed in the depths like lights in a swimming pool at night.

Due to the still sizeable Alaskan and Siberian runs, pinks are the most numerous salmon on the face of the globe. In 1926 I.F. Pravdin observed a massed run of Asiatic pinks in Kamchatka that was nearly a mile long, and made a roar "somewhat similar to the noise of boiling water in a gigantic cauldron." Besides their small size, prominent hump and white belly, several behavioral characteristics set pinks apart from other salmon. They always return to their natal streams as two-year-olds, and in Washington, which is the southern extreme of their range, they are the only salmon that run exclusively in odd numbered years. And apart from chum salmon, they are the only salmon that immediately seek salt water after hatching.

Although not generally numerous elsewhere on the Olympic Peninsula, pinks have long thrived in the northern rivers that flow into the strait (the Elwha alone had a pink run of more than 250,000 fish prior to the construction of the dam). Here the rivers are agreeably short, the steep valleys somewhat fortified against predators, and the rivers less likely to flood and scour the eggs out of the redds. In striking contrast to the Queets and the other rain forest valleys on the west side of the peninsula, the area around the Dungeness receives less than seventeen inches of rain a year. This climatological quirk is caused by the central mountains of the Olympic Range, which interrupt the flow of moisture off the Pacific and cast a rain shadow across the region. The Dungeness is one of the few places on the Olympic Peninsula where cactus and ponderosa pine grow naturally alongside salal and Douglas fir.

Glancing down at my watch at 9:30, I saw a star reflected in the pool below, and decided it was time to go. I played the flashlight beam across the curving tail of the glide where I would be walking to avoid disturbing the fish too much, and then switched the light off. The darkness welled up like blood from a bad wound. I could make out the black line of trees along the far bank and the mountains silhouetted against the starry sky, but nothing else. Concentrating on my feet, I found the gravelly riverbed strewn with large round rocks. Planting my staff, taking a step, planting my staff, taking a step with the other foot, I slowly waded thirty-five yards out into the rushing, shin-deep water, imagining each caress of the current to be a salmon.

Finally, when I judged that I had reached a point near one of the most active redds, I switched the light back on. There were many more salmon on the glide now, and almost all were in motion. Some dashed away from the yellow beam, others seemed dazed by it. A tremendous fight between two females erupted to my right where the wake from their repeated thrashings rocked along the shore for the entire length of the glide. A small female who had not yet spawned slipped by me so close that I could see that her dorsal fin was capped at the terminus of each ray with a series of jewel-like shields that glowed pink on the upper edge, and gold on the lower. Beyond, six large Chinook moved upstream in single file through the melee like sharks among pilot fish. Several of these Chinook had large patches of white fungus on their heads from trying to get through the hatchery weir downriver.

Pink salmon are given to group sex, which can involve as many as six males spawning at the same time with a single female. Typically, spawning occurs when the female swims slowly over the nest, and then lowers her anal fin into the redd, stimulating the nearby male or males. As her consort joins her on the redd, both fish gape and quiver violently while the eggs and sperm are shed simultaneously into the waiting bowl of gravel. I did not get a chance to observe the penultimate moment in the life of pinks that night, but I did see what might be described as a moment of compassion. Off to my left a hideous old male whose face had been broken away just in front of his eyes was holding near a still-prime female on her redd. The female, who had several active suitors, not only tolerated but almost seemed solicitous toward her spent and dying companion, and it occurred to me that he was probably a former mate.

On the way back, I stopped again near a large boulder and turned on the light for the last time. Salmon all around me flew off in unison like arrows from a squad of archers, but two males remained. One of them hung right in front of me, rolling his back toward me whenever I shone the light directly at him. Just as I was admiring how cleverly he was diminishing the intensity of the light, the other fish, who had a prominent white stripe down the crest of his hump, swooped down on me from behind. Feeling a sharp tug at my leg, I found this bold cavalier had locked himself onto my right boot, and was trying to shake me. As I raised my staff to dislodge him, the other fish attacked my left leg. It was then that I noticed that I was standing in the middle of their redd, and stumbled away toward camp.

Forty-two thousand summer pinks returned to the Dungeness and Graywolf rivers in 1979. This was considerably less than the run's historic high of 400,000 fish, but still better than the 8,000 fall pinks that returned to the lower river one month later. The reason for the difference in size between the two pink runs in the Dungeness system is largely due to the availability of water. The early run, which is genetically distinct from the later run, enters the river in July when snow melt has swelled the flood and made passage to the headwaters relatively safe. The fall run, by comparison, enters the river in September and October when it is fed almost exclusively by irrigation seepage, and spawns immediately at the mouth. In the old days, the Dungeness could accommodate both in profusion (and may have even had more late fish than early), but today both the river and the runs have been altered.

Captain George Vancouver, who commanded the second European exploring expedition along the north coast of the peninsula in 1792, was so impressed with the beauty of the Dungeness that he named it for a sentimental favorite that flows into the English Channel near Dover. "The country before us exhibited everything that bounteous nature could be expected to draw into a single point of view," he wrote. "The land . . . was well covered with a variety of stately forest trees. These, however, did not conceal the whole of the country in one uninterrupted wilderness, but pleasingly clothed its eminences, and chequered the valleys . . . which produced a beautiful variety of extensive lawn, covered with luxuriant grass, and diversified with an abundance of flowers." Vancouver's lawn was actually a series of prairies that the Klallam Indians kept cleared with fire, and which baked into a desolate waste every summer while the damp forest luxuriated all around.

White settlement began on the Dungeness a half century later at Whiskey Flats, which took its name from the proprietors' policy of selling liquor to the Indians. About this time the Klallam Indians were forced to abandon their three villages at the mouth of the Dungeness, and move down onto the beach. It was here that the Klallams suffered the last epidemic of the white diseases that had turned their land into "a slaughterhouse of human beings" as early as 1791. David Douglas (for whom the Douglas fir is named) wrote of the effect of the subsequent "intermittent fever" on the Indians of the Northwest: "Villages, which had afforded from one to two hundred effective warriors, are totally gone; not a soul remains. The houses are empty and flocks of famished dogs are howling about, while dead bodies lie strewn in every direction on the sands of the river." Twenty years later the Klallams were struck with smallpox when a sailing ship bound from San Francisco to Seattle lost most of its crew to the disease en route. As the ship drifted down the Strait of Juan de Fuca, the survivors threw the clothes and bedding of the dead overboard. These items washed ashore and were picked up by the Indians, who died like flies in the winter of 1855.

The Treaty of Point No Point, signed that year, gave the United States title to the land of the Klallam. In exchange, the tribe was to receive a reservation, money and the right to continue to live their traditional salmon fishing life. Although the promised money was never forthcoming, the whites became increasingly anxious to remove the Indians from the area. Finally, after the Klallams murdered a dozen Tsimshian Indians camped on Dungeness Spit on the night of September 21, 1868, federal troops were sent to burn the Klallam villages at Port Townsend and Diamond Point, which was quickly turned into a leprosarium. All Indians who could be found were towed in their canoes down Hood Canal behind the government cutter to the reservation at Skokomish. The few Indians who managed to remain in the Dungeness area were forced to pay $500 in gold for 210 acres of logged-off land at the place they named Jamestown.

Meanwhile, early white settlers in the Dungeness, like Shetland Island sea captain Thomas Abernathy, began building their crude log cabins and clearing the forest of Douglas fir, noble fir and western red cedar. Some of the timber was cut and sold for shipment to San Francisco, but most of it was simply burned. "The timber of the eastern portion [of the peninsula] has been largely destroyed, either by axe or by fire, mainly by the latter," a U.S. Geological Service report observed in 1902. That same year, on September 12, the Northwest experienced its famous "Dark Day," when 110 forest fires raged simultaneously from the Canadian border to central Oregon. Smoke from the fires was so heavy that no more than a twilight gleam pierced the clouds all day, and many "thought the world was coming to an end, and prayed for deliverance," as an Olympic Peninsula school teacher recalled.

Potatoes, oats and peas were planted among the stumps, and early yields were so heavy that the Dungeness quickly became one of the principal exporters of agricultural products in western Washington. New settlers pushed the clearing to the edge of the prairies around Sequim, and into the hanging valley in the foothills of the Olympics ten miles from the strait. Whiskey Flats changed its name to Dungeness, and a group of farmers built a three-quarter-mile-long dock at the mouth of the river, which facilitated the loading of freight and forever eliminated the common tideflat sight of a woman "with her voluminous skirt and petticoats that swept the floor, hat with flowing veils, and kid gloves, being carried by a barebacked Indian."

Prosperity seemed assured, but even as the early agricultural achievements were transforming the valley, they threatened its future as well. John Muir was one of the first to note that the presence of water is as much a result of the forest as the forest is a result of water. "The thirsty mountaineer knows well that in every Sequoia grove he will find running water, but it is a mistake to suppose that the water is the cause of the tree being there," he wrote in 1894 in *The Mountains of California.* "On the contrary, the grove is the cause of the water being there. Drain off the water, and the trees will remain, but cut the trees, and the stream will vanish." Contemporary records are inconclusive, but it appears that the destruction of the forest eliminated much of the surface moisture from the Dungeness in this fashion, for after the turn of the century, irrigation was required to farm the areas that had produced crops so freely when the settlers first arrived.

Although not as grandiose as Thomas Aldwell's scheme for the Elwha, the idea of diverting water from the Dungeness to irrigate the land around it became a similarly consuming passion for Dungeness farmer D.R. Callen. When the first water from the river flowed onto the parched farms around the Sequim Prairie in 1896, the settlers made "offerings" to the irrigation company he founded, one of which featured local children reciting a poem composed for the occasion ("A laurel wreath to honor those good men/ Who brought about this glorious end,/ So in the future there may be those/ Who sees this land blossom like a rose"). Soon half a dozen irrigation companies were draining the river into an elaborate network of gravel troughs and wooden aqueducts, and the valley had become a leading dairy center with a combined herd of 9,000 cows.

If irrigation was a godsend for the farmers of the Dungeness, it was something less of a boon to the river's wild salmon. Jerry Angiuli, a member of the Clallam County Planning

Commission, remembered how after flood irrigating in the 1940s he had to "go through the fields picking up salmon because the cows would leave an area of grass the size of that desk there around the dead fish. . . . There were hundreds every year, mostly pinks and cohos." Despite some farmers' efforts to save as many of the fish as possible, Angiuli recalled that large numbers of adult and juvenile salmon were lured to their deaths in the irrigation system, and that irrigation activities downstream from his family's farm eventually exterminated the once numerous salmon of Cassalery Creek, which flows into the strait a little more than a mile east of the spit. Altogether, more than a dozen distinct runs of pink, coho and chum salmon were removed from the Dungeness area in this manner.

Apart from entrapment, irrigation affects salmon by reducing the amount of water in which they can effectively spawn and rear. A shrinking world inevitably means fewer salmon, but as the size of a river decreases, it also changes its basic nature, becoming warmer and less hospitable to salmonids. Higher temperatures reduce the amount of oxygen the water can hold, and make possible the speedy growth of diseases and predators. The water that returns from irrigation ditches is warmer still, and often contains manure and pesticides, which further rob the water of oxygen and weaken the fish that survive. Agricultural activities are the reason why more than a dozen of Washington's major rivers do not presently meet state water quality standards, according to the state Department of Ecology's 1978 annual report.

With the passage of the National Land Reclamation Act of 1902, small scale irrigation projects like the one on the Dungeness gave way to a massive series of public works dams and diversions extending across Washington, Oregon, Idaho, Montana, Nevada and California. In arid eastern Washington, the U.S. Bureau of Reclamation built five dams on the Yakima River between 1910 and 1933. These impoundments were designed to store water for the orchards in the lower Yakima

Valley, but in the process they completely wiped out the Yakima River sockeye, the single largest run in the river, and reduced the total Yakima salmon run from an estimated 600,000 fish in the nineteenth century to a combined total of 9,000 fish today.

The Truckee River in western Nevada was the site of another early Bureau of Reclamation project. The first American explorers into the Sierra Nevada Mountains found a giant race of cutthroat trout, *Salmo clarkii,* in Pyramid Lake on the Truckee twenty miles from present day Reno. "Their flavor was excellent, superior, in fact, to any fish I have ever known," wrote Lieutenant John C. Frémont in 1844, adding that "they were of extraordinary size—about as large as Columbia River salmon." The Pyramid Lake trout continued to flourish and feed the Paiute Indians (who practiced a first salmon ceremony similar to the Quinaults') until 1905, when the bureau built Derby Dam on the river to divert water for irrigation. Thirty years later, the largest race of cutthroat trout in the world was rendered extinct because Derby Dam would not release enough water to let the fish reach their spawning grounds.

Grand Coulee Dam, which the Bureau of Reclamation built during the late 1930s, was at once the boldest engineering feat ever undertaken by man, and the single most destructive human act toward the salmon. When Lewis and Clark passed down it to the Pacific in 1805, the Columbia River produced more Chinook, coho and steelhead than any other river in the world. Although it had been overfished by white commercial fishermen for nearly five decades, the river still supported substantial runs of all species when the bureau decided to build an unladdered dam across the immense glacial outwash in eastern Washington known as Grand Coulee. As on the Elwha, fisheries authorities hoped that hatcheries would compensate for the effect of the dam, and once again the hatcheries failed and the runs were lost. In the end, Grand Coulee Dam closed more than 1,000 miles of salmon rivers and streams, and altogether eliminated the choicest spring and "June Hog" summer

Chinook that had previously been the mainstay of the commercial fishery.

In areas where salmon remain, the Bureau of Reclamation has continued in the spirit of Derby Dam. On the Yakima River, for instance, the bureau's Tieton and Bumping Lake dams have shut off all water when salmon were trying to spawn downstream several times during the last decade. And in 1979 the bureau killed nearly six million kokanee, or lake-dwelling sockeye, when the reservoir behind Tieton Dam was emptied to provide irrigation water for farms. According to Neil Modie in the *Post-Intelligencer,* "most of them were sucked at high speed through an outlet tunnel at the dam and were spit into a pool below it. They died either here or farther down the Tieton River, battered to death in the . . . flowing water. . . ."

The man who has run the Bureau of Reclamation for the last three decades is Floyd Dominy, a born westerner whose Stetson is white, and whose "belt buckle is silver and could not be covered over with a playing card," as John McPhee observed in *Encounters with the Archdruid.* Although he got his start working with the small farmers of Campbell County, Wyoming, Dominy has been responsible for a general failure to enforce portions of the National Reclamation Act designed to help the small, independent farmer. Section five of the act required that all beneficiaries of federally funded irrigation projects be residents on the land, and own no more than 160 acres under subsidized irrigation. On the seventieth anniversary of the original bill's passage, the General Accounting Office reported to Congress that so many abuses of section five had occurred under Dominy and his predecessors that the intent of the act had been foiled.

Writing in *Not Man Apart,* Brian Berkey described how illegal empires of publicly irrigated land have been amassed as a result of the bureau's ten-dam Central Valley Project in northern California:

> One such sale, approved by the Bureau of Reclamation in 1974, involved deeding 3,000 acres from Giffen, Inc. to 12 dif-

ferent names, trusts, and companies; the deal also included an additional 5,000 acre lease agreement. Through either lease or sale, all the land ended up under the control of Jubil Farms, Inc., whose "farmhouse" is in mid-town Manhattan; the sole incorporator, or "farmer" is the middle-aged secretary of the legal firm that put the deal together. The total of 8,000 acres — 12 square miles under federally subsidized irrigation—is currently farmed as one unit, and its income goes to the Japanese trading company which owns Jubil Farms and financed the whole thing.

The water for Jubil Farms, Inc., comes from the Sacramento River, where salmon were burned on the banks at the base of a dam in 1921, and where a government survey in 1938 found not one effective fish screen on diversions used for power or irrigation, and many without effective fish ladders. "Numerous laws on [California] books dating from 1870 . . . called for protection of the runs," Netboy wrote in *The Salmon: Their Fight For Survival,* "but actually the streams could be legally dried up by water users, thus making ladder laws unenforceable." Another report prepared by a blue-ribbon panel for the California Legislature in 1971 found that the salmon of the Sacramento-San Joaquin basin had declined 65 percent since the completion of unladdered Shasta Dam, the crown jewel in the Central Valley Project.

On the Dungeness, irrigators and water speculators secured a "legal right" to three times as much water as the river actually contains under a ruling of a Clallam County Superior Court judge who divided 500 cubic feet per second of water between dozens of claimants fifty years ago. The Dungeness River contains an average of 130 cfs above the irrigation diversions, and 45 cfs below; irrigation removes 85 cfs, or roughly two-thirds of the river. Like California, Washington has long required "that a flow of water sufficient to support game fish and food fish populations be maintained at all times in the streams of the state." "Unfortunately," according to a report by the U.S. Attorney's Office on enforcement of fisheries law, "this policy has not been implemented. There is legislative authority to establish 'minimum flows required to protect fish life,' but minimum flows have been established for only one river, the Cedar . . . [and this] is being challenged judicially."

The U.S. Attorney's report blames the existence of "potentially very destructive" irrigation practices in Washington on the state Department of Ecology. "Although the departments of Fisheries and Game have submitted thirty-four requests [for legal recognition of the salmon's right to water] in ten years, the Department of Ecology has acted on only one. Meanwhile applications for water rights other than fish are being filed, and these have priority by the time they are established." Under Governor Dixy Lee Ray, the Department of Ecology expanded its anti-conservation role, opposing Fisheries and Game on other important battles for salmon on the Skagit, Chehalis and Columbia rivers.

During Ray's first year in office, the irrigation companies withdrew so much water from the Dungeness River during the hot summer months that the early pink run could not ascend the river to the canyons on the Graywolf. Unable to secure more water for the fish, the Department of Fisheries sent bulldozers down into the dry bed of the Dungeness in a last ditch effort to scour a narrow channel for the fish to use on their way upriver. The ploy worked well enough to save the majority of the run, but no similar solution could be found for the fall pink run, which arrived six weeks later. Thousands of the fall-run fish piled into the lower Dungeness and died without spawning because they could find no suitable place, were picked off by predators in the shallows, or were overcome by the diseases that accompany warm water and crowded conditions. Before long, the stench of their rotting carcasses could be smelled a mile from the river.

Low flows were only part of the wild fall pinks' problems though, for instead of "blossoming like a rose," the Dungeness had grown a variety of common urban blight. There are still a few successful dairy and cabbage seed farms in the valley, but much of the choice irrigated agricultural land is being transformed through the magic of real estate offerings. "For Sale/ Small Acreage/ Easy Terms," "Acreage View Tracts For Sale," "Open House/ Condominiums/ House Sites," the bright signs among the quaint abandoned fields proclaim. Driving through the valley, the signs tell the story of the area's present development: "No Trespassing," "Keep Out," "Beware of Dog" (in fluorescent orange letters on black), "No Trespassing," "Sold," "Hay/ Baled and Standing," "No Parking," "View Lots" (amid bare, eroding soil and stumps), "Posted/ No Hunting/ No Fishing/ No Trespassing," "For Sale," "Watch For Flying Golf Balls," "For Sale," "No Trespassing/ Violators Will Be Prosecuted" (beside a mailbox painted with red and yellow flowers in a meticulous hand).

A victim of the virtual West Coast monopoly of California produce made possible (if not necessary) by the Bureau of Reclamation projects in the Central and Imperial valleys, the Dungeness is being subdivided and sold to a mushrooming community of retirees, who are drawn by the sun and spectacular setting. "Here's how it works,"Angiuli said, pushing back his hat and putting his feet up on the desk in his Sequim tire store. "The realtors like to sell five-acre ranchettes. A guy and his wife go out to look at the property on a sunny day when the mountains are out and the strait is blue, and he's got to have it . . . The first year is OK — especially if he retired early and spent some time on a farm as a kid — because he's busy building his house and having the lawn put in. Then he's got a house and four-and-one-half acres of weeds. So the second year he builds a fence and buys a cow. Then he finds he's got to have a stall to breed her, irrigation and a tractor to plough the land, and the next thing you know he's got $30,000 into his 'hobby' farm. Then one of his friends says, 'heh, there's great fishing out at Sekiu. Let's go out for a few days.' But he can't do it, because someone's got to take care of the place, and the next thing you know he starts getting real mad, and decides he's going to subdivide his place into little lots. . . . When someone

tells him he can't do that, he calls his lawyer and starts screaming about his rights."

Much of the development has taken place within the flood
plain of the river, that is, within the area normally flooded
every few years. When the inevitable has occurred, the new
homeowners have clamored for dikes, which have further reduced the salmon's chances of survival. In 1973, for instance,
Clallam County asked Dungeness Farms for permission to
divert the river so that some new homes would not be flooded
at high water. "They put the diversion across the river in 1974,"
recalled Polly Ball of the county's Shoreline Advisory Committee, "but the first high water pushed the river right over the
diversion, which left the old channel high and dry, and prevented the salmon from using what I understand was one of
their best spawning grounds." The departments of Fisheries
and Game have jurisdiction over permits for structural flood
control projects, but they did not even check into the matter far
enough to see that no engineer had ever approved the project.
The U.S. Attorney's report cites severe short-staffing and insti-
tutionalized timidness as the causes of the departments' failure
to act in situations like the one at Dungeness Farms. "The
departments are concerned that if many [river degrading] projects are denied, their authority might be reduced," it observed
dryly.

A growing population has also increased the fishing pressure
on the Dungeness. All of the Dungeness and Graywolf have
routinely been closed to pink fishing by whites since the 1960s,
but in fact they are fished heavily by "sportsmen" and local
subsistence fishermen, along with Klallam Indians. When I was
on the Graywolf on August 23, 1979, I found several parties in
the Dungeness Forks Campground engaged in illegal fishing.
One man in his thirties was showing his son how to gut a pink
female he had snagged with a three-barbed hook and spinner
setup. The hooks had caught the still silvery female just in
front of the tail, which now bled on the black rocks. The man

turned the fish over so that her brilliant belly faced up, then inserted the knife, slitting her open and hacking out her gills. Neither the Department of Fisheries nor the U.S. Forest Service, which has jurisdiction over the area, had posted signs notifying people in the campground that the pink run was closed for conservation of the run.

Further up the river, I found the tails of three salmon that had been severed with a knife, and another pink salmon female that had been gutted and abandoned to the soft ball of maggots now unfolding on her tongue. Around dark, a crew of seven or eight hardy-looking types arrived in camp, and set out for the river with snagging gear and beers in tow. "Lots of salmon up here," one of them called amiably as they passed my tent. Noting four pinks laid out on the grass by their trucks in the morning, I stopped and learned that they were Forest Service timber cruisers. Just then, another member of their party returned with the rest of the morning's catch: three female pinks weighing four or five pounds apiece.

That same week, a supermarket in Port Angeles was advertising slender, four-pound coho for $4.50 per pound whole, or $18 for a fish that would barely feed two hungry men.

Island Imports

HAZEL HECKMAN

Hazel Heckman's move from her native Kansas to western Washington and then to Anderson Island in lower Puget Sound has resulted in two books: Island in the Sound, *from which this excerpt comes, and* Island Year. *Heckman is also the author of* Boots and Forceps, *about her brother's life as a country veterinarian.*

Students of natural systems may be interested to learn that the slugs featured in this piece are themselves imports. The native slug species prefer decayed vegetation to fresh and are not serious garden pests.

Any isolated community, I suppose, would serve as a prime example of coexistence. But it has been said that nowhere so much as on an island is the relationship between all of its organisms, both animal and vegetable, so close and so apparent. I remember with chagrin an abortive effort on my own part, a few summers after our arrival, to meddle with that admirable interdependence here.

I suppose the most maligned wobbler of Mother Nature's balance wheel in the Pacific Northwest would be the misguided Scot (if Scot he was) who is said to have brought from his native heath a handful of broom seeds, to plant in his Oregon dooryard or on the Nisqually prairie where he was (allegedly) employed by the Hudson's Bay Company. Perhaps the Englishman who is said to have imported the first pair of starlings would rate at about the same level.

My own interference occurred, innocently enough, when I attempted to introduce two dozen Kansas hoptoads to the dubious delights of Island living. Unlike the mistaken Britons, I was not prompted by nostalgia. Nor was it I, precisely, who imported them. Actually, the toads were the fault of Ezra Taft Benson, the then Secretary of Agriculture, and my niece Barbara, a biology student at the state college in Manhattan, Kansas.

The affair began with my having received in the mail a government bulletin entitled *Slug Control.* I have always been a sucker for government bulletins, especially for those of the agricultural variety. My bookcases are stuffed with them. If someone with authority takes pains to write a thing, and the busy printing office in Washington takes the trouble to put it into type, and my congressional representatives compiles a list which I may have gratis, I feel duty bound to order the maximum allowable.

Motivated by desperation, I read this one with avidity. Previous to the time that we took up "small farming" on the Island, as the bulletin facetiously described our dawn-to-dark labors those first years, I had yet to encounter a garden slug. On many a "dew-pearled" morning, as a child, I had watched the slug's cousin, the shell bearing *Gastropoda*, a rather charming mollusk that wears a decent covering, creep across "the thorn," and I had collected many a matchbox full of his delicate abandoned shells. I still recall my feeling of revulsion at the first sight of his slimy relatives, *Deroceras* and *Limax*, on the Island here.

My notion of the worst of all possible worlds, I can say without reservation, would be a planet on which the common garden slug predominated. Whereas I avoid stepping on a beetle and will go to great pains to capture a house spider and carry him outside, I can, and frequently do, scissor slugs in half with a malevolence that shocks my family.

From the time the dews and damps set in of early evenings until the grass dried off of mornings, from long before lilac time in the spring until frost, our bit of earth here was literally carpeted with these repulsive, slow-moving creatures, in three colors — black, brown, and unpleasantly mottled.

Like the hoptoads, which seemed for a brief and happy time

an answer to the slugs' depredations, they are nocturnal feeders. They can be found during the day, nestled cheek by jowl, in moist places — under boards or rocks, in crevices in the earth, underneath piles of trash, hidden in the root crowns of plants, especially of the blade variety, or plastered cozily against the underside of large protective leaves such as chard or rhubarb, or (the baby ones) glued to the ventral side of the one lettuce leaf you neglect to examine before tossing it into the salad.

That summer, slugs were more prevalent than usual. I set rows of cabbages and marigolds and went out the following morning to find quarter-inch stems or no trace of my labors at all. I planted expensive seeds and the sprouts disappeared as they broke crust. Slug bait, a commercial product made from apples, took its toll by the hundreds. But it was as though fresh and hungry slugs arose, phoenix-like, from the slime of their dead companions.

Even before *Silent Spring*, I was something of an organic gardener. Having grown up in the sulphur and coffee grounds, ladybug and red pepper era, when the only pesticide we knew was Paris green, which we used on potato beetles but nonetheless mistrusted, I was always on the lookout for natural remedies. *Deroceras*, according to the bulletin, had few enemies, because, understandably enough, few creatures could stomach him. The sole exception named was the common hoptoad, which was endowed with some mysterious enzyme for rendering the slimy secretion that marks the slug's passage not only digestible but palatable.

I mentioned the interesting fact about the toad's digestive system, I remembered afterward, the following autumn during my annual visit back on the farm in Montgomery County, Kansas, where, just as during my childhood, a grandfather toad, fattened on sowbugs and the like, lived among his lesser relatives in the cellar drain.

On a Sunday evening preceding my April birthday the next spring, I ferried back to town frustrated after two days of "small farming" spent, largely, in a vain attempt to save a few rows of seedlings from the ingestive inroads of the common garden slug. I entered the house to the sound of the ringing telephone and sprinted up the steps to answer.

"This is the post office," a reproachful male voice informed me. "We've been trying to reach you all day. We've got a special delivery air mail package of live frogs for you."

"Sorry," I panted. "Wrong number."

"Is your name Heckman?" the voice asked sharply.

I admitted that it was.

"Then I've got a package of live frogs for you," he insisted. "I'll be right out to deliver them." I heard the lonely sound of the dial tone.

When I opened the front door several minutes later, the uniformed gentleman who confronted me looked mildly relieved, having half expected, I suppose, that the recipient of live frogs might appear astride a broomstick, or at least with a black cat in the offing. He handed over a small cardboard box, conspicuously labeled LIVE FROGS RUSH PERISHABLE, and covered with airmail stickers. "I think they're dead," he said, all reproach again. "I've not heard a peep out of them since morning."

Because it had been literally thrust at me, I accepted the package. "I'm sure there must be some mistake," I said. "What would I want with live frogs?"

My question went unanswered. Having done his duty, the postman disappeared in the night. I heard the diminishing "pop, pop" of his cycle.

I carried the box, at arm's length, to the light. Unmistakably, it was addressed to me. The return address was that of a biological supply house in Topeka, Kansas. Mystified, but curious, I set the box on the table and took a knife from the drawer. Having cut the tape, I lifted the flaps.

On top of a dampish mass of newspaper lay a card, with the message: HAPPY BIRTHDAY FROM BARBARA. As I pondered this, an ugly head emerged, followed by a pair of long legs. Not a frog, but a toad! It seemed an answer to almost prayer when I had absorbed the connection. I shoved the animal back and clapped the lid shut.

The box on my lap, I sat down to think. For a toad's skin to dry out meant death, I had read somewhere. The newspapers in which my friends (probably a pair) were swathed were only slightly damp. They would be thoroughly dry by morning. The poor things had already been confined for twenty-four hours in the small box, which smelled, definitely, toady.

I set the now-silent container on the table and dialed an acquaintance who, I knew, had worked in a biology lab at the University of Washington during her student days. "Why don't you put them into the bathtub with a little water?" she suggested, when she could stop laughing.

Fortunately, Earle was not at home. I was all alone in the house. Who would mind . . . or know, for that matter? In the bathtub, they would have life-sustaining water, and freedom of a sort, until I could get them across to the Island.

In the bathroom, I ran an inch of water into the drain end of the tub. In the other, I constructed a little island of damp crumpled paper. I set the box carefully in the tub and again, more cautiously this time, lifted the flaps.

Like the animals from the ark, or, more aptly, like the clowns in the small-car circus routine, toads emerged. I readjusted my estimate to two pairs, to four, to a half dozen. And still they came. One by one, they broke cover, flexed long-cramped muscles, and leapt at the porcelain walls of their new prison. They fell back with soft wet plops, and leapt again. I gave up trying to estimate their number. It was like attempting to count a plate full of Mexican jumping beans. The tub was alive with toads, all jumping and splashing at once in a grand jamboree.

When they had stopped coming, I took the newspaper out of the box. A last toad lay, belly-up, at the bottom. But, like the delayed-action jester, he came to life at a touch. Thoroughly soaked now, or exhausted, the others gradually ceased their leaping and flattened themselves on the floor of tub so that I was able to count them. I counted twenty-five, a baker's two dozen!

During the night I awoke again and again to the sound of soft guttural croaks from the bathroom, and was obliged to orient myself. In the morning, the weakling, or I supposed it to be he, lay belly-up again. The others appeared content in their new white world and quiet, until I began to gather them up to return them to the close confines of their shipping box, which I had filled with fresh paper.

It took a while to corral them all. Just as I thought I had a firm grip on a slippery captive, he would slide through my fingers and be off as though on springs or by jet propulsion. I caught one by the hind legs as he went over the side. Another made the shower head in two leaps, where he perched like a warty gargoyle and allowed me to brush him into the box. I took up the "dead" one to carry him to the trash bin.

Recruiting strength and momentum, he uncoiled his legs, negotiated the kitchen in a series of leaps, and disappeared through the door into the living room. Minutes later I hauled him, palpitating, from beneath the sofa and restored him to his companions, burrowed, by now, silently into the depths of their unfragrant container.

Nor did they utter a single croak during the long drive to the ferry slip. "I've got a box of hoptoads here," I told obliging Peter James. "I wonder if you'd take them up the hill during your morning layover and turn them loose around the garden."

"Now, I've heard *everything*," he said. "Do you want me to catch some flies for their lunch?"

"They'll do fine on their own," I told him smugly. "They're going to live on garden slugs."

All the same, I felt a sense of almost maternal responsibility for their welfare. That afternoon, I called a commuting Island friend, a teacher, to ask whether she would mind stopping by the Island house on her way home, "to fill the bird baths." "I've sent over twenty-five hoptoads," I said. "They just might take off for the pasture pond unless there's water handy."

"How's that now?" she asked. "For a second there, I thought you said *hoptoads.*"

When the phone rang the following morning, the awakening began. "Don't ask *me* to water your toads again," she opened indignantly. "I've still got a queasy stomach. I met a snake at your gate last night with a toad head-first down his gullet, and still kicking!"

"Didn't you even rescue the toad?" I wailed.

"I turned green and fled," she said. "I was completely shattered."

Chamber of Commerce brochures from west of the Cascades invariably point to the fact that this area contains but one snake, a harmless nonpoisonous *Thamnophis* of the grass or garden variety. I had seen a few in the garden and had welcomed the sight, knowing that they accounted for a good many harmful insects. I should have remembered, alas, that all *Kansas* snakes, including *Thamnophis*, were also inordinately fond of amphibians. I remembered that a bull snake had taken over the cellar drain one summer, depleting the toad population there. It was only when he was accidentally dispatched that they made a comeback.

I hurried to the Island the following weekend, resolved to account for every snake I met. Actually, I never accounted for but one. And then I was riddled by the feelings of guilt that invariably follow my taking any life, save that of a slug (I cannot explain this). He was stretched full-length on the rock wall, taking the sun, and I struck in a fit of umbrage.

Previously, as I say, I had seen a *few* snakes around the place. The following spring, word must have gone the rounds of the snake world that a CARE package had arrived. One week, I counted five snakes, the next, seven. I saw more snakes that summer than I had previously seen on the Island, and more than I have seen any summer since. They lay about in the sun, suspiciously fat, and thrust out their tongues when I approached too close. One took up residence underneath the foot scraper at the back door and emerged on warm afternoons to lie on the sidewalk.

Occasionally, I saw a Kansas toad. One passed his days in a

little aperture underneath an ivy-covered piece of driftwood at the back, from which he emerged of evenings to flick beetles off the sidewalk with his incredibly swift tongue. Slugs emerged, too, from underneath the selfsame bit of drift, and headed for the cold frame, leaving trails of slime behind them. So far as I could see, Toad failed to notice them. I could only conclude, charitably, that he remained blissfully ignorant concerning his own peculiar enzymes. He was, after all, a native Kansan.

To tell the truth, we *did* note a certain abatement of slugs that summer. And, although I dislike to contemplate the theory, the Kansas toads may have been indirectly responsible. One night, Toad failed to appear. Nor was he in his "Hall" when I looked there, hopefully, each following day for a week.

Something like a week later I came suddenly upon what seemed an abnormally large *Thamnophis* zigzagging his way across the ivy. Positive that here was Toad's assassin, and incensed, I raised my hoe to strike.

A shadow fell across the sidewalk. "I wouldn't do that if I were you," my neighbor Murph, a seasoned Northwest gardener, admonished mildly. "That's one of your best friends, you know. Accounts for more garden slugs than all the bait you can pour out of a box."

I lowered the hoe. "You don't *mean* that?" I gasped.

"Darnedest thing you ever saw. They eat slugs the way you'd eat peanuts. I read somewhere they secrete some kind of acid that breaks up the slime."

I watched the serpent disappear with a flick of his tail in the heather. "Maybe," I muttered, "you read it in a government bulletin."

"Might be," he agreed. "But I doubt it. I don't often read 'em . . . Only other critter I've ever seen would touch a slug was a big Indian Runner duck I had once."

I tried *that* panacea, too, a few summers ago. And, by George, he was right. One warm afternoon I stopped at Lake Florence, a lovely jewel of a lake on the highest portion of the Island, for a dip in the swimming hole. I was surprised to see a big white duck with a broken wing being pursued in and out of the water by excited children.

Whom did he belong to, I asked. He must have escaped from somewhere. A newcomer, driving in, volunteered the information that she had seen just such a duck at the R's house.

It seemed unlikely that a bird with a broken wing could have come so far, I thought. But, if the children would help me catch him, I would take him there.

By the time we had reached the R's, we were close friends, the duck and I. For all of his considerable bulk, he insisted upon riding on my lap, where he kept up a constant chatter as he nibbled at my earlobes. Certainly he was someone's pet, and a lovable one. I drove into the R's driveway feeling like a Scout who had done my good deed for the day.

I was unprepared for Mr. R's not-so-very-pleased look. "He *was* our duck," he admitted. "I took him to the lake this morning to get rid of him. But thanks all the same. Just leave him and I'll take him back there."

"No such thing," I told him, considerably embarrassed. "I'm going that way. I'll just drop him off."

"If you're sure it'll be no bother."

"Did you raise him?" I asked, lifting my voice so as to be heard above the duck's loud protests.

"Mrs. G. gave him to me," he said. "Someone gave him to her children as a duckling. She got so she couldn't stand his slug-eating habits, so she brought him over here and gave him to us. But he makes such a mess . . ."

On the drive back, as though he sensed that he was about to be abandoned again, the duck grew even more loving. Dropping his voice to a husky little-more-than-whisper, he poured his woes into my ears, the while he billed them. "If you do this," he warned, "I'll not last the night, with all the 'coons around. To-morrow you'll find my bones and feathers in a heap on the bank."

I slowed for the lake turn all right, but could not bring myself to make it. "But I *can't* take a *duck* home," I argued. "What would Earle say? We're only week-enders now. We can't be hauling a big hunk of poultry back and forth. And what would I do with you in town?"

"Just let me out of the car in the driveway, behind the hedge," he said, finally, "and let *me* handle it."

I was upstairs changing into dry clothing when I heard Earle's shout. "There's a *duck* here. Where in thunder do you suppose he came from?"

"A *duck*?" I echoed. I leaned from the window to look. Earle was squatted on the sidewalk. The duck stood tall in front of him, talking in his sibilant pianissimo, the while he nibbled lovingly at his master's earlobes.

We kept him for two months, until cold weather. During the week away, I prevailed upon Ellen's granddaughter Cindy to feed him and put him away each night in one of the poultry houses and to let him out in the morning.

It would be difficult to say, in that time, how many slugs he accounted for. Perhaps he did not eat slugs at all when we were away, only the corn with which we provided him. I have a notion that he may have eaten slugs only to show off, or to secure his position. I grew extremely fond of him, as did Earle. When we drove into the driveway on Friday evening, he came to meet us, relating the news of his week's activities.

During the day, he sat on the patio, a soft white mound of feathers, with his head tucked out of sight completely. This required, naturally, a good deal of scrubbing. But he was worth every ounce of energy expended, and I think he knew it. Step outside the door, and he was on his feet in an instant, his head going up and down on his long neck, his soft voice imploring you to bend down so that he could express his affection.

Following a prolonged session of that, he moved off toward the orchard, his head still bobbing, the while he coaxed you with many a backward look to accompany him. We took profitable and pleasasnt walks together, he and I, lifting boards and turning over leaves to expose the long fat cigar-shaped slugs which he consumed with apparent relish. One day, by actual count, he ate twenty-one.

His crop was so distended and heavy that it dragged in the grass as he made his way to the plastic baby tub that served as his water basin. There he stood, blowing bubbles in an effort to clear his bill of the gluey slime that had all but cemented the two parts together. At such times, like his former owner Mrs. G., I turned away from the sight. But, following alternate periods of dunking and blowing, and honing on the grass blades, he emerged with his bill as bright and beautiful as ever.

When we went East for an extended business trip in the autumn, I was obliged to find a home for him. "Just for the winter," Earle promised. "We'll bring him back in the spring when we move to the Island for the summer."

But the new owner, a tidy housekeeper, was appalled by the mess he made and passed him on to another party, where, I fear, he may have served as a Thanksgiving *pièce*. I refrained from asking. In any case, he was gone from the Island, and from the earth, probably.

But, in fond memory, I still see him assemble himself as if by magic from a heap of sleeping feathers, to greet me with his gentle persuasive monologue as we set off on a slug hunt. In the moments when I can bear to contemplate his probable end, I cannot help wondering if he tasted a trifle peculiar, and whether the resultant gravy may have had a slightly "epoxic" consistency.

The Farmer on the Land

RICHARD WHITE

This study of the effect of farming on a native island community is excerpted from Land Use, Environment and Social Change, *by Richard White. The book is an environmental history of Island County, Washington, concentrating on Whidbey Island. Professor White teaches history at Michigan State University, East Lansing.*

Americans have celebrated the frontier farmer as, among other things, a bearer of "civilization," a founder of new communities, and a conqueror of the wilderness, but the farmer served one purpose that they have usually neglected. Along with the explorer and trader, the farmer composed the vanguard of the ecological invasion of North America. He introduced to the continent, both intentionally and accidentally, the exotic plants and animals that have permanently altered the natural systems of the New World. Some farmers, at least in Island County, explicitly recognized their ecological function. As Walter Crockett, an early settler, wrote [in an 1853 letter], the main object of the farmer in settling new land was:

> . . . to get the land subdued and the wilde nature out of it. When that is accomplished we can increase our crops to a very large amount and the high prices of every thing that is raised heare will make the cultivation of the soil a very profitable business [sic].

Subduing the land and getting the "wilde nature out of it" meant replacement of native flora and fauna on a massive scale. Crockett and his neighboring farmers did not begin the ecological invasion of Island County. The European diseases that had riddled the Salish, demoralizing and destroying them, and

the potatoes and beans that the Indians had brought to the islands before the whites arrived had already invaded and altered
the Salish ecosystem. Farmers did not initiate the assault on the
natural world of the Salish, but they increased its scale and mag-
nified its consequences.

Changes in the natural environment by the Salish had basically
involved shifts in the proportions of native flora and fauna. Of
necessity Salish land use had consisted of the manipulation of a
set number of native plants. Some plants had diminished, others
had increased. American farmers attempted something entirely
different. Their first fields were beachheads for exotic plants:
wheat, oats, barley, peas, corn, cabbage, carrots, turnips, beets,
tomatoes, melons, squashes, parsnips, and a host of others. The
survival of these plants depended on the farmer just as surely as
his survival depended upon them.

The process of invasion seemed at once simple and straight-
forward and laborious and tedious to men like Crockett. The
farmer would clear existing "useless" vegetation and replace it
with useful vegetation. He would eliminate wild herbivores and
introduce domestic herbivores. He would plow up bracken and
plant wheat. He would eliminate elk and introduce cattle. When
he was done, wild nature would be gone and a farm would be established. Ecologically this view may have been dangerously
simpleminded, but in the nineteenth century as well as in the
twentieth, this outlook remained common.

Like the Salish before them, the farmers created their own
landscapes. But since the farmer undertook more ambitious
changes than the Salish ever had, the consequences were more
far-reaching, the interrelationships more complex, and the
chances for miscalculation far greater. The arrival of the white
farmer spurred what one botanist [George Neville Jones] has
described as the most cataclysmic series of events in the natural
history of the area since the Ice Age.

The farmers came to the county as part of the much larger
Oregon and California migrations of the 1840s and 1850s.
Americans had spilled north of the Columbia River, entering the

Puget Sound region by the mid-1840s and settling on lands the British had believed they would retain when diplomats determined the final status of the Oregon country. The Americans found these lands less fertile and less inviting than those to the south, but they nevertheless came in sufficient numbers to undermine British hegemony. The land north of the Columbia became American, not British, and by 1854 these lands formed the base of the new territory of Washington. But the migration into the Puget Sound region remained a mere rivulet when compared with the rivers of people that flowed to Oregon's Willamette Valley.

The first white farmer to arrive in Island County came in 1850. Isaac Neff Ebey, then thirty-two years of age, had been born in Ohio during what amounted to a pause in the life-long migration of his Pennsylvania-born parents. He went with them to Illinois in 1832 and afterwards to Missouri. In Missouri Ebey married and fathered two sons before going on alone to the Oregon country in 1847. Briefly diverted to California by the gold rush, he came north to Olympia on Puget Sound and then to Whidbey Island. In 1851 he sent for his wife and children. Parents, brothers, sisters, cousins, and in-laws followed. Besides the Ebeys, other extended families came to Whidbey. The Crocketts, Hills, Millers, and Alexanders all brought friends, old neighbors, and in-laws to settle and to dominate the county. Settlement was never random; the census of 1860 shows that one-third of the settlers on Whidbey Island during the 1850s had been born in New York, Pennsylvania, and Virginia. They arrived in a burst of settlement that continued from the late summer of 1852 to the late spring of 1853. In the fall of 1853 the white population of the county was 195. It would rise to only 294 by 1860.

These people settled almost entirely on the prairie land. By the early 1850s Whidbey Island had already gained a reputation as the "garden spot of Oregon," the best agricultural land in the Pacific Northwest, or at least in what was to become Washington Territory. Even men so skeptical of farmland of the Puget Sound region as to compare it with the notoriously poor land of New

England exempted Whidbey Island. For a moment the island landscape and the settlers' interests coincided. The prairies had attracted these men, and they covered the prairies with claims that followed the natural boundaries of the land. By the spring of 1853 little unclaimed prairie land remained on the island.

. . . .

The tools that these settlers used to make their roads, farms, and villages were not impressive. But as the Salish had shown, far-reaching effects can be obtained from relatively unsophisticated technology. When Isaac Ebey's estate was inventoried after his murder by Canadian Indians, his farming equipment consisted of a set of double harnesses, a breaking plow, a cast iron plow, a harrow, four hoes, two picks, two shovels, and two scythes, the whole valued at $79. These tools, along with the axe, the maul, and the adze, were the instruments with which white men sought to conquer the land.

Except for the plow, the tools the American farmers brought to the land did not differ drastically from those of the Salish. At the time of white settlement, the two peoples differed not so much in technology as perception. Americans reduced the complex view of the Indians to a few simple categories. The new farmers saw most native plants as simply "weeds" or "brush." Land that grew these plants was, in the words of the census, "unimproved." Land on which native plants had been eliminated and replaced by domestic plants was "improved." For all practical purposes most native plants vanished from the everyday landscape of the new settlers, disappearing into the undifferentiated flora of the prairies. The intimate and detailed knowledge of the natural world that was widespread among the Salish became a specialized realm of esoteric knowledge among the whites.

The settler's perception of the natural world and his technology found symbolic expression in the fence. The utilitarian function of the worm or snake fence was obvious: It enclosed crops and kept cattle out. The fence became both an actual and a symbolic boundary line. It separated improved land from the Salish prairie, and it also marked the boundary of the farmer's conscious control. To the settler this fence seemed the natural division that the river was to the Salish. The fence reduced the prairie to human size, and within its boundaries the farmer replaced the ecosystem of the prairies with the cultivated field or the permanent pasture.

The fence also marked the line between two different kinds of perception. Inside the fence the farmer observed closely; he was inquisitive and experimental. But outside the fence the farmer's perception narrowed. He took only limited interest in the undifferentiated "brush" of the prairies. He left knowledge of most native flora to specialists. One of these specialists was James Swan, ethnologist, Indian Agent, and botanist. Swan's own interest in the natural world was catholic, taking in both the "useful and the useless." His descriptions of the prairies are unique in their specificity.

> The ground over which we walked was a perfect carpet of flowers. Conspicuous among these were the beautiful rhododendron with its rich cluster of blossoms, the blue flowers of the camonass, the bright red of the bartsia and columbine. The white blossom of the fragrant seringa, the variegated lupine, the purple of wild peas and iris intermaking a floral display equal to any I ever witnessed in California and one that would delight the heart of every true lover of nature [sic]. [*Scenes in Washington Territory, No. 9*]

The farmers recognized the beauty of these prairies, but beauty was expendable. They sought utility. When Swan sought uses for native plants, farmers could appreciate his concerns. They were sympathetic when Swan attempted to promote the nettle as a plant that could be domesticated and made into a source of fiber, or when he reported to the Smithsonian on the attempts of a farmer in Whatcom County to domesticate native grasses. In Island County farmers took a similar if limited interest in wild plants that might find a market. A brisk trade in wild cranberries

(*Vaccinium oxycoccus L.,* var. *ovalifolium* Smith) developed, so
brisk that attempts were made to domesticate and cultivate them.
And Rebecca Ebey did begin to domesticate the wild gooseberry
(*Ribes* L.) by the simple expedient of uprooting a young bush and
replanting it within the confines of her garden. But of the hundreds of plants known by the Salish, relatively few, besides trees,
had economic value for the whites. Cattle grazed wild grasses
and farmers cut them for hay; settlers picked several kinds of
berries, and pigs ate the camas. The remaining native flora, outside the forest, was useless — mere brush and weeds — and
Swan's curiosity about these plants remained foreign to most
American settlers.

The farmer treated the world outside the fence differently
from the world within, and different treatment yielded different
results. Plowing was the first, and most significant, alteration
that the farmer made in the land within the fence. But when in
March, before the first flowers bloomed, the farmer's plow bit
into the prairie, the dense root network of the bracken fern often
snagged and stopped it. As Walter Crockett wrote, bracken
made the land "quite hard to get into cultivation." It was quickly
learned that only heavy breaking plows drawn by four or five
yoke of oxen could cut through these roots. Oxen, however, because they were essential not only for land breaking but also for
logging, were in much demand; they were expensive and hard to
obtain. In 1852 the Crocketts offered oxen for sale at $150 a
yoke. A year later Isaac Ebey wrote that oxen cost $300 a yoke,
and the same year Nathaniel Hill had to go all the way to Olympia to buy a yoke for $205. If a man could not afford to buy oxen
at these prices, he might hire them. Isaac Ebey estimated in 1853
that men with oxen and breaking plows could contract to break
1,000 acres of Whidbey prairie that spring and summer at from
$10 to $15 an acre. But the hired teams never appeared, and little
land was broken.

Bracken roots made plowing the prairies slow and laborious,
but even worse, plowing did not kill the roots. When split and
turned under by the plow, the rhizomes promptly sprouted.

Crockett guessed in 1853 that it would take four or five years of cultivation to eliminate the fern, but thought that it would not damage the crops. Even in the late 1850s Winfield Scott Ebey complained of bracken in his father's wheat and potatoes, and this was on land that had been under cultivation since 1852 or 1853. Throughout the century bracken would remain in fields planted to timothy, and its presence in hay reduced the value of the crop.

Plowing was necessary for farming, but it had consequences the farmer never intended. When settlers turned under acres of bracken and grass, they were destroying the native cover of the prairies. Evaporation rates then increased and water needed during the dry summer months was lost. Repeated plowing broke down the granular texture of the virgin soils that enabled them to retain water, thus reducing the water-holding capacity of the soil still further. The results of this process varied from one soil type to another. The soils of Ebeys Prairie continued to produce well year after year, but the Townsend Loam soils of north Penn Cove, which initially produced quite well, suffered a cumulative degradation during the nineteenth century. The amount of water retained by these soils declined until most crops grown on them suffered from lack of moisture. From being the most productive soils in the county, they deteriorated until by the twentieth century they could only be used for pasture.

The effects of new environmental conditions upon the imported plants were as hard to predict as the eventual consequences of plowing on prairie soils. Every movement of farming peoples into new areas changed the rules of farming because physical conditions changed. Not all the plants farmers brought with them flourished. In each new region farmers began afresh, and they had to discover from experience the limits of the new land and climate. So it was on Whidbey Island.

During the first decade of settlement farmers tried, and failed, to produce plants that ranged from such semi-tropical species as the eggplant and tomato to the pioneer staple, corn. A letter Nathaniel Hill wrote home on his way to Whidbey Island in 1852 requesting, among other things, tomato, gumbo, melon, sweet potato, and eggplant seeds, shows the deficient understanding some early farmers originally had of the climatic conditions of western Washington. The cool summers and long, wet winters of the region doomed any plant requiring either a long, hot growing season or warm summer nights.

Once climate had winnowed potential food crops and those suitable to the conditions of western Washington had been selected, farmers seem to have shown no particular attachment to the crops they had grown in other places at other times. In Island County there was no strong correlation between the farmer's place of birth and the crops he grew. Farmers from the middle Atlantic states and Virginia, the leading grain producers of the period, did tend to raise more grain than other Island County farmers, but farmers from New York and Pennsylvania, the leading potato producing regions of the 1850s, actually tended to raise fewer potatoes than county farmers in general. Even in wheat and potato production, the relationship was a modest one and can obviously be the result of many causes outside of place of birth, especially since many of these men had moved several times.

Once the farmers had discovered the limitations of climate, markets largely determined what they produced. In the 1850s villages, logging camps, crews of ships, and the military provided a ready market for nearly any crop the farmer chose to raise. High prices were paid for grain, potatoes, and hay throughout the decade. Flour sold as high as $20 per 100-lb. barrel on Whidbey in 1853 and $16 a barrel in Olympia in 1858. In the 1850s markets left farmers free to grow almost any crop climatically suited to the region. On Whidbey Island they concentrated on three staple crops: potatoes, oats, and wheat. In their uneven experience with these crops lies an illustration of some of the complexities of crop selection on an agricultural frontier.

The Salish had grown potatoes on Whidbey Island since 1840, and the Indians and the British supplied American settlers with their first seed potatoes. These potatoes were tasty, but very small, and almost immediately the settlers began to import larger strains from California. Potatoes became the most widely grown crop on the island. In 1860, 50 percent of the farmers planted them and produced crops ranging from 20 to 4,000 bushels, with 70 percent of the farms producing from 20 to 500 bushels. In a sense, the potato supported early white settlement in much the same manner corn did elsewhere. Already adapted to the climate and soil of the country, small acreages produced large yields. With either wild meat or salmon as a source of protein, it formed the bulk of the setters' diet, one almost identical to the staples of the Salish.

The American settlers themselves introduced oats to the prairies, and the plant seems to have adapted to the environment as quickly and easily as the potato. In the 1850s neither farmers nor newspapers mentioned any particular problems with the crop. In terms of bushels produced, oats were the second largest crop in the county in 1860, and in terms of acres planted, they probably ranked first.

Of the triumvirate of staple crops, only wheat failed to adapt to the prairies. On Whidbey during the 1850s, farmers constantly expected bumper crops of wheat, and they were just as constantly disappointed. Isaac Ebey called the first wheat crop sown in the spring of 1853 the most promising crop he had seen in the Oregon country. When harvested, however, yields proved uneven: Walter Crockett obtained twenty bushels to the acre, but Nathaniel Hill, less than a mile away, had a total crop failure. For the rest of the decade consistent wheat yields proved unattainable. Indian war and blights (probably smut) accounted for some of the difficulties, but even in years with no social, economic, or ecological upheavals harvests were disappointing. By 1860 only 16 percent of the farmers in the county produced 200 bushels or more of wheat, and 60 percent of the farmers in the county produced no wheat at all.

Why wheat was not successfully raised is unclear. The climate was suitable; farmers on Whidbey Island would later claim world record yields. There was an ample market for wheat at high prices. Failure probably stemmed from a combination of factors: lack of rain following late spring planting, competition from bracken, lack of a suitable wheat strain, and contamination of at least part of their seed wheat with smut. Furthermore, the botanist for the Railroad Expedition who visited the islands in the mid-1850s attributed difficulty with the crop to an excessively fertile soil that caused the wheat to grow rankly and subsequently lodge, or fall over. But not matter what its cause, the failure of wheat to adapt to an environment apparently well suited to it demonstrates the sometimes mystifyingly thin line that separated the success or failure of a new crop in a new land.

The inability of some desirable crops to adapt was one side of the farmer's problems with ecological imports; the other side was his almost total inability to prevent the entry of unwanted invaders. Weeds are an inevitable result of any human attempts to restrict large areas of land to a single plant. But what is often ignored is that many common weeds are not native plants, but, like the farmers and the crops they cultivate, invaders from Europe. Current ecological opinion holds that most European weeds are plants that have developed a close association with man. They are adapted to open land and, without the intervention of men, open land rarely occurs in nature. Floods and fires are the only other forces that produce it.

By plowing the prairies and by cutting roads, man opened the way for invasion by these weeds. In New Zealand, H. Guthrie-Smith could watch the annual movement of the invaders along the roads from ports where they had arrived. There was no Guthrie-Smith to chronicle the invasion of Whidbey, but settlers in the 1850s noticed that invaders appeared largely in fields and along the roads. The fields, where a single species maintained by human labor had replaced a complex natural community, became an especially easy target for invaders.

The introduction of weeds into a new area was usually accidental. Seeds adhered to men or their vehicles; the seeds of weeds were mixed with crop seeds or dispersed among packing materials or the ballast of ships. In 1865 Granville Haller, who owned a farm near Oak Harbor, examined 391 lbs. of seed wheat. He estimated it to be one-third wastage, "barley, oats, buckwheat, and peas besides an abundance of cheet and smut." By 1855 many common European, North American, and South American weeds had established themselves on the islands. European foxtails (*Alopecurus carolinianus* Walt. and *Hordeum* L.) and shepherd's purse (*Capsella bursa-pastoris* (L.)) moved in on roadsides and spread to other open lands: abandoned gardens, fields, and overgrazed prairies. The sow thistle (*Sonchus oleraceus* L.), a competitor with food plants in cultivated fields and gardens, was already a troublesome weed at the time of the Railroad Survey in 1853–54, and American black nightshade (*Solanum nodiflorum* Jacq.), now an ubiquitous weed in the Puget Sound region, was at home in cultivated ground. Another invader, knotweed or willowweed (*Polygonum lapathifolium* L.), was also a garden weed, but it did not adapt as well as its companions. Dock or sorrel (*Rumex acetosella* L. or *Rumex crispus* L.) had appared in cultivated sections of the prairies, and it had the capability of spreading outward along roads onto relatively undisturbed lands where it eliminated other, more valuable species. All of these were troublesome and harmful, but Canadian thistle became by far the most damaging.

Canadian thistle (*Cirsium arvense* (L.) Scop.) apparently reached Whidbey Island in the spring of 1856, probably mixed with crop seed. When settlers discovered and identified the plants, they undertook an immediate campaign of eradication. The Davises of Ebeys Prairie apparently had the heaviest infestation, and they took the lead in trying to destroy the thistles. By the spring of 1857 it looked as though they had been successful. However, before the plant had been recognized, a farmer named Stewart had taken a single stock of it and cultivated it for its flower. He let the plant go to seed, and that fall or winter he abandoned his claim and his garden. By June when W.S. Ebey visited the claim, he found that the garden was "litterly [sic] covered with it (thistles)," and the seeds had already ripened. Ebey cut the stalks and burned the garden, but it was too late; the plant was securely established. Undoubtedly later additions to the thistle population were made, but from the beginning the plant became one of the most harmful weeds on the island. Spreading both by seed and by its underground root network, it damaged both cultivated and pasture land. The failure of the settlers to control the thistle held a warning of how, once begun, ecological change could prove irreversible.

On the prairies, outside the fences, the ecological impact of settlement was the result not of plowing and planting, but of rooting, browsing, and grazing by domestic animals — especially pigs, cattle, and sheep. John Alexander imported the first bargeload of domestic animals to Whidbey Island in 1852. The arrival of cattle helped spark the eruption of worm fences that soon covered the prairies, but cattle ruined unfenced Clallam potato fields. As the importation of exotic animals progressed and cattle and hogs destroyed more and more Salish food plants, the coexistence of the Salish and white systems of land use became increasingly difficult. Only the rapid decline of Salish population prevented a direct clash.

Oregon's Legislative Innovations

LEGISLATIVE RESEARCH, BEVERLY MARCH

This report, prepared at the request of the Oregon legislature, was published in 1975.

This report describes areas in which Oregon has adopted innovative legislation. The following list includes (1) laws which appear to have had no counterpart in other states at the time of their adoption; and (2) laws which appear to have been adopted in Oregon at almost the same time as in another state.

VOTER REGISTRATION

Oregon was among the first states to require registration of voters on a statewide basis. In 1899 the Legislative Assembly passed a law directing the county clerk of each country to register all electors. However, the law also contained provisions enabling persons to vote who had not registered.

INITIATIVE AND REFERENDUM

Oregon's initiative and referendum measures were proposed by the 1901 Legislative Assembly and approved by a vote of the people in 1902. Though Oregon was not the first state to enact such measures, its electorate was the first to use the initiative and referendum powers.

VOTERS' PAMPHLETS

In 1903 Oregon became one of the first states to provide for the printing and distribution of voters' pamphlets to the electorate. The 1903 law directed the secretary of state to produce, for each voter, a pamphlet containing the title and text of each ballot measure. In 1909 the Legislative Assembly passed a law requiring that pamphlets include information on candidates and that separate pamphlets be printed for each party on primary elections. In 1975 the law was amended to provide for the production of one combined pamphlet (containing information on both parties) in primary elections.

DIRECT PRIMARY

In 1904 both Oregon and Wisconsin enacted direct primary legislation on a statewide basis. Oregon's law was the first to provide for a closed primary, which requires voters to declare party affiliation at the time of registration. (Wisconsin's law was the first provide for an open primary, which allows voters to select the ballot of either party on election day.)

DIRECT ELECTION OF U.S. SENATOR

In 1906 Oregon became the first state to elect a U.S. senator by a vote of the people. Direct election of senators was provided for in the 1904 primary election law. Prior to that time, senators were elected by the Legislative Assembly. In 1913, with ratification of the thirteenth amendment to the U.S. Constitution, direct election of senators from all states became mandatory.

RECALL

In 1908 Oregon became the first state to provide for the recall of public officials by the electorate. The recall provision, created by constitutional amendment, was the result of an initiative petition.

PRESIDENTIAL PREFERENCE PRIMARY

In 1910, through initiative petition, Oregon became the first state to enact a presidential preference primary law—allowing the electorate to express its preference for presidential and vice-presidential candidates. Oregon was among the first states to provide for direct election of delegates to the national nominating conventions.

PUBLIC ACCESS TO BEACHES

In 1967, with passage of the "beach bill," Oregon became the first state to declare sovereignty over the ocean shore existing within its borders. The law designates the entire shore, except for portions specified in the statute, as a "state recreation area" which is to be preserved and maintained by the state for public use.

BICYCLE PATH FUNDING

In 1971 Oregon became the first state to earmark state funds for the establishment of bicycle trails. The law requires that at least one percent of state highway funds be expended annually for the construction and maintenance of bicycle trails and footpaths.

BAN ON NON-RETURNABLE AND PULL-TAB
BEVERAGE CONTAINERS

In 1971 with passage of the "bottle bill," Oregon became the first state to prohibit the sale of non-returnable beverage bottles and cans. The law, which also bans pull-tab cans, applies to beer, malt liquor, mineral water, and carbonated soft drink containers. Since 1971 bottle deposit laws have been adopted in three other states — Vermont, Maine, and Michigan.

DECRIMINALIZATION OF MARIJUANA POSSESSION

In 1973 Oregon became the first state to decriminalize possession and use of marijuana. The law provides that persons convicted of criminal possession or use of drugs involving less than one ounce of marijuana are guilty of a "violation" punishable by a fine of not more than $100. The 1974 Special Session amended the public promotion statute to create a similar "violation" for persons convicted of criminal drug promotion involving less than one ounce of marijuana. Since 1973 California, Colorado, Maine, Minnesota, Ohio, South Dakota, and Vermont have also decriminalized possession of small quantities of marijuana.

50-MILE STATE FISHING ZONE

In 1974 Oregon became the first state to extend its jurisdiction over marine fisheries to 50 miles. The bill to extend such jurisdiction was originally passed by the 1973 Legislative Assembly, but vetoed by the governor. It was repassed in 1974 over that veto. Subsequently, Congress has enacted legislation extending U.S. jurisdiction to 200 miles off the coastlines.

FLUOROCARBON BAN

In 1975 Oregon became the first state to ban in-state sale of aerosol cans using chlorofluorocarbon compounds. The law became effective March 1, 1977. In 1977 the Legislative Assembly passed a bill exempting aerosol sprays used for certain medical purposes from the ban.

Energy 1990

GREG HILL

In the summer of 1976 the Seattle City Council voted after months of study not to buy into two proposed nuclear power plants, a decision which the plants' subsequent history has made to seem increasingly prescient. Greg Hill is a Seattle writer and civic activist. He wrote his analysis of the Energy 1990 decision, which appears here in a condensed version, in 1978 when he was a Ph.D. candidate in political science at the University of Washington.

THE ORIGIN OF THE ENERGY 1990 STUDY: SUPERINTENDENT VICKERY, CITY LIGHT AND SEATTLE PROGRESSIVISM.

In the spring of 1975, representatives of City Light appeared before the City Council to ask approval of an option to buy 10 percent of the output from two proposed nuclear power plants. Under the proposed agreement with the Washington Public Power Supply System (WPPSS), which was formed to coordinate the financing of projects too expensive for a single utility, City Light would finance a portion of the construction and operating costs in return for a commensurate share of the output once the two nuclear plants were operational — sometime in 1984. According to City Light planners, the utility's load growth could be expected to increase by 3 to 4 percent per year, and a share of the output from the nuclear plants would be essential in order to meet the city's growing demand for electrical energy.

At the Council hearings, City Light's request for nuclear power was supported by representatives from some of the most powerful organizations in the area. John Ellis, vice president of Puget Power, argued that nuclear power would be the cheapest way of meeting rising demands over the long run, and Donald Covey of the Downtown Development Association warned that failure to buy into the nuclear plants would jeopardize Seattle's future job climate. Meanwhile [on April 24], the Seattle *Times* ran an editorial arguing that nuclear power was in the "national interest, the regional interest, and the city's own interest," and that without the proposed plants "looming power shortages could cause industrial shutdowns and loss of jobs." Criticism of City Light's request for nuclear power came mostly from environmentalists who questioned City Light's demand projections, pointed to the dangers of nuclear power, and raised concerns over further deterioration of the environment.

Although the agreement placed before the Council by City Light did not require an irrevocable financial commitment by the city, it did require a quick preliminary decision if City Light was to retain its option to participate in the nuclear plants. Because of the urgency, the Council unanimously approved City Light's request to enter into the option agreement. However, because the financial commitment was so great — City Light's share could cost over $250 million — and the issue so complex, the Council asked for further study of Seattle's future energy needs, alternatives, and impacts.

In the meantime, the Washington Environmental Council (WEC) filed a lawsuit seeking to invalidate the Council's approval on the grounds that the city had not filed an Environmental Impact Statement (EIS) concerning the nuclear plants. The *Times* was rabid, calling the lawsuit [in a June 4 editorial] "another environmentalist barrier to needed energy," and accusing the WEC of resorting to "irresponsible legal and political tactics to block the development of domestic energy resources." Others responded more calmly, however, with officials from City Light and the Office of Policy Planning (OPP) proposing that a consulting study be done concerning the issues at stake. Pete Hennault and Dan Barash from City Light and Jerry Allen of OPP prepared a study strategy which involved citizen participation, an independent consultant, and an Environmental Impact Statement. In exchange, the WEC withdrew its lawsuit, and the Energy 1990 study was begun.

Although the City Council had already asked for an independent energy study, the WEC lawsuit was crucial in providing bargaining leverage to City Light Superintendent Gordon Vickery's critics, both in shaping the study, and, perhaps more important, in the selection of individuals to the citizens' committee which would be responsible for monitoring the consultant's report. The call for bids on bonds to finance the nuclear plants had already been postponed because of the lawsuit, and there was the possibility of a further legal challenge, since some WPPSS money would be used to help finance Puget Power's Skagit nuclear project, perhaps violating the state constitution's prohibition against lending credit to a private corporation. However, while the WEC lawsuit posed the immediate threat to Vickery's plans, there was a further circumstance which figured in the development of Energy 1990 — the legacy of public power in Seattle.

City Light occupies a special place among the bureaucracies which make up Seattle government. A municipally owned utility, it has often been at the center of local, and even regional, politics. City Light's marvelous success in bringing Seattle residents the cheapest electricity in the country has endeared it to nearly everyone. Coupled with the practical benefits of low rates and, until recently, free repairs, City Light has also been a source of civic pride in Seattle as the leading public utility in the United States. More recently, though, City Light had become, as the Energy 1990 process would later reveal, the major institutional focus for many concerns about technology, employment, and the quality of the environment. Together, the legacy of public power in Seattle and the stakes of future energy decisions had produced a growing public interest in the question of City Light's acquisition of expensive nuclear power.

It is against the background of these high expectations that one can look back to the beginning of the Vickery regime and begin to understand the erosion of Seattle's acquiescent good faith in City Light. A large part of that erosion had nothing to do with Gordon Vickery but rather with an exceedingly important economic circumstance: City Light had reached the end of an era of declining cost curves. In 1971, two years prior to Vickery's nomination as superintendent, increased operating costs had forced City Light to ask for its first rate increase in fifty years. And since that initial increase, there have been two others — one in 1974 and another in 1976. Moreover, because City Light had virtually exhausted the capacity of its hydroelectric generating base, any additional capacity necessary to meet new demands would probably involve thermal generation at a cost ten times that of hydropower. Besides the consumer activism that these rising electric rates would eventually produce, there was already in existence a well-organized environmentalist challenge to City Light policies. Among other things, these organizations had been critical of City Light's promotional pricing, which encouraged the consumption of electricity, and which, in turn, would eventually require additional generating plants in order to meet rising demands....

It is difficult to say whether the program of citizen involvement initiated by Vickery in 1973 was aimed directly at winning public acceptance in this new context of doubts and criticism. Vickery's own position as superintendent was weakened by virtue of the close 5 to 4 vote over his confirmation on June 12, 1972 and more recently by the threat of a strike at City Light. There is no doubt that he was aware of the legitimating effects of citizen participation in City Light policy-making, for he noted in the 1976 *Annual Report* that "when people take part in setting the objectives, they're far more likely to help meet them." Perhaps Vickery had hoped that the 1990 study would, if not co-opt his environmentalist critics, at least convince the wider public that, as he put it, the "days of cheap power are over." [*Times*, June 4, 1975]. But whatever Vickery's motives might have been, the important point to bear in mind is the unique character of

City Light and its relation to the public . . . .

When Pete Hennault and Dan Barash of City Light met with Jerry Allen of OPP to formulate the Energy 1990 study, they decided upon a strategy which included the three essential components mentioned above: citizen participation, an independent consultant, and an Environmental Impact Statement. It was a response entirely consistent with the principles and sentiments of Seattle's resurgent progressivism.

An independent forecast of Seattle's future energy requirements was dictated in part by the growing suspicion of load forecasts done by utility planners who had an interest in the outcome. Just as an earlier progressivism had sought to wrest policy-making authority from "interested" politicians and place it within independent bureaucracies, this new wave of progressivism hoped to wrest an essential decision-making resource from the now politicized City Light bureaucracy through the use of an independent consultant. In a complex area like energy policy, information is power, and as the [June 13] *Argus* put it, the utility's "monopoly on information (was) about to be broken."

Those who planned the Energy 1990 study had high expectations of the consultant's independent forecast of Seattle's future energy demands, even beyond its hoped-for legitimating role. To city planners, an independent forecast offered the prospect — and perhaps the only prospect — of rational decision-making on an issue fraught with both technical complexity and a fundamental conflict of values. On the one hand, there were difficult technical issues concerning the relative merits of nuclear as opposed to coal-fired generating plants, of the impact of rising energy costs on the growth of the demand for electricity, and so forth. On the other hand, the question of nuclear power was inextricably connected with another set of issues concerning environmental quality, economic growth, and, more generally, the sort of city Seattle was going to be. Each of these issues, it was originally hoped, would somehow be taken care of by the consultant's report.

Besides involving an independent consultant and an Environmental Impact Statement, which would impose a format of public hearings and other requirements on the process, Energy 1990 called for a citizens' committee that would monitor the study for "completeness and validity." Like the independent forecast, the formation of a citizens' committee was partly dictated by City Light's declining credibility. In a broader context, however, citizen participation fitted well with Seattle's new civic activism. In fact, the expectation that some form of public involvement will accompany major policy decisions in Seattle is so widespread that one city planner was led in retrospect to remark that "nobody does anything in Seattle these days without citizen participation."

Actually, Energy 1990 called for two citizens' committees, a body of thirteen to participate in the selection of the independent consultant team which would do the study, the Citizens' Selection Committee (CSC), and then an expanded body of twenty-seven which would monitor the consultant's report, the Citizens' Overview Committee (COC). The two committees, selected within the constraints imposed by the quest for public credibility, had the same basic composition, consisting, in approximately equal proportions, of environmentalists, advocates of economic growth, and representatives of various civic organizations. Two further characteristics of the committees stand out: first, their members were nearly all professionals, including lawyers, economists, business consultants, administrators, and academics; and second, many of them represented or were in some way affiliated with important organizations in the area, including the Washington Environmental Council, the Sierra Club, Friends of the Earth, the Downtown Development Association, Roofers and Waterproofers Local #54, Pacific Northwest Bell, the Western Environmental Trade Association, the Chamber of Commerce, the Association of Washington Business, the King County/Snohomish Manpower Consortium, the League of Women Voters, Seattle Pacific College, Metro, Seattle University, Neighbors in Need, Allied Arts, and the University of Washington. With an independent team of consultants and considerable staff support from City Light and OPP at its disposal, the COC would prove to be a formidable agent in the 1990 process.

The first impact of citizen participation was in the selection of an independent consultant. This was an extremely important part of the entire process, first, because everyone had placed such high importance on the forecast itself, and second, because it was widely known that there were a number of consulting teams who shared the standard utility perspective. The Citizens' Selection Committee initially ranked the consultant proposals, inter-viewed the top rated applicants, and, after a final ranking, sent their recommendations to Superintendent Vickery. Although Vickery had objections to the committee's selection of Mathe-matical Sciences Northwest (MSNW) to do the forecasting, a compromise was reached and MSNW was selected as part of a three-member consulting team to do the Energy 1990 report. The citizens' preference for MSNW was apparently based upon MSNW's intention to develop an econometric forecasting model in contrast to the traditional utility method of historical trend-ing . . . .

The person responsible for developing the load forecast was Dr. Donald Shakow of MSNW. Shakow had formerly been an economist with a Seattle food co-op, an association which no doubt brought him into contact with any number of unconven-tional ideas. And it was not long before he began to question the standard utility assumptions, in particular City Light's premise concerning the sale of surplus power from the nuclear plants at full cost. According to the option agreement with WPPSS, City Light would have to pay for its full share of nuclear generation regardless of whether its customers needed the additional power. City Light, in turn, assumed that any surplus could be sold to other utilities at full cost, thereby avoiding the need to raise its rates (which would further dampen demand) in order to cover its share of the costs. Shakow questioned whether the surplus could in fact be sold at full cost, and developed another set of as-sumptions concerning surplus sales, assumptions which had the effect of reducing the forecasted rate of load growth and hence the need for nuclear power. Vickery, however, apparently realized these implications and insisted that Shakow stick with the original assumption. Shakow was prepared to resign when word of the conflict reached the COC and the City Council. At this point Vickery could only compromise, and it was decided that Math Sciences would do two forecasts — one with the City Light assumption of selling the nuclear surplus at cost, and one with the assumption of selling part of the surplus power below cost. Having selected the independent consultant, the citizens' committee had now interceded to insure his autonomy.

This was the first of two significant changes made in the original study proposal in which the COC played an instrumental role. The other involved the development of a number of future energy scenarios. According to the original proposal, the consultants were to make a preliminary presentation on energy requirements one month after the beginning of the study, following which Superintendent Vickery was to choose one alternative for further study. The COC, however, became concerned that City Light's selection of a preferred alternative would jeopardize fair consideration of a number of energy futures. And Vickery, by this time preoccupied with the strike at City Light, again conceded; a number of alternative energy scenarios would be selected for equal consideration. Thus, the COC was not only maintaining the consultant's independence but was also, by this time, shaping the contours of the study itself.

CITY LIGHT: AN ORGANIZATION IN CONFLICT

The conflict in Seattle between advocates of nuclear participation and their environmentalist critics had a rough analogue within City Light. The utility, according to a former City Light economist, was divided between "traditional growth-minded engineering managers on the one hand and, on the other hand, new pressures and personnel dedicated to a challenge of conventional utility wisdom" [(Seattle) *the Weekly,* June 9, 1976]....

That conflict intensified because the issues being raised by Energy 1990 brought into question the very purpose of City Light, which up to then had been to provide a cheap and plentiful source of electric power for the city. Each faction had both an ideological and an organizational stake in the answer to that question; whether City Light would shift its focus from increasing supply to managing demand was not an issue about which either side could be at all indifferent.

The consultant's preliminary report, distributed in October, was full of implications threatening to the old guard. The load forecast showed a much lower rate of growth than the original City Light forecast, due in large part to the effect of increasing electricity prices in dampening the demand for electricity. To those involved with power management the preliminary findings posed two threats: one organizational and the other psychological. At the lower forecasted rate of growth the need for new power generation would be minimized, and the resources made available to those engaged with power generation would likewise decline. And, to add insult to injury, behind the innocuous notion of an elastic demand for electricity loomed a less innocuous assumption, that the public would be unwilling to buy power at higher prices and would even reduce consumption. It must have been a difficult claim to accept for a generation of engineers who took pride in the fact that Seattle consumed more electricity per capita than anywhere else in the country and for whom the heavy consumption of electricity signified not wasteful excess, but freedom from drudgery.

The issue of surplus sales contained similar implications, only with a wider application. It was one thing to forecast a slower rate of growth in Seattle, which had already undergone its experience of "city building." It was quite another thing to suggest that the rest of the region would forego the experience of growth so that a surplus of nuclear power could not be sold at cost to other utilities in the area. Nevertheless, the elasticity of electrical energy demand had greatly diminished the prospects of new generation, and the veterans responded by withdrawing from the 1990 study, leaving the process to proceed in isolation from the old guard at City Light.

THE POLITICAL ECONOMY OF LOAD FORECASTING AND THE SPECTER OF NON-GENERATION.

It is through the load forecast that a utility determines what future demands are likely to be. It is the starting point of City Light planning, initiating a sequence of decision-making which involves nearly all the major organizational units within the utility....

In the past, when City Light was developing its hydroelectric capacity, its planning was predicated upon a declining cost curve. Once its generating and distribution system was in place, additional units of energy were less costly to produce — at least until existing capacity was exhausted and new facilities had to be constructed. In this era of declining cost curves, inflated load forecasts were not only self-fulfilling, they were also a matter of policy. Excess capacity was not a problem, since surplus energy was relatively cheap and could be easily marketed. As a matter of fact, it was City Light's widely supported aim to produce a surplus of cheap energy in hopes of attracting new industry to Seattle. Within this context of "city building," then, the forecast deliberately incorporated a strategy of providing cheap surplus power, the use of which was actively promoted by City Light.

With the near exhaustion of City Light's hydroelectric capacity and the alternative of much more expensive thermal power facing the utility, load forecasting entered an era of rapidly rising cost curves. The high cost of additional generation placed a new set of constraints on load forecasting, with severe penalties for erring on either the high or low side of actual demand. A low forecast, and consequent underbuilding, would perhaps result in shortages, industrial shutdowns, and a loss of jobs. A high forecast, on the other hand, would lead to overbuilding and require significant rate increases to pay for unutilized capacity. It was for these reasons that much of the 1990 debate focused upon the differences between the City Light and the MSNW forecasts.

City Light's request to buy into the nuclear plants was based upon a forecast prepared by its economist, Doug Woodfill, which extrapolated historical trends of energy use into the future. This method of forecasting, called "trending," had been the traditional utility practice until recently and is full of judgmental considerations. Woodfill's forecast projected an annual growth rate in energy sales of 3.7 percent. Given the lower growth rate for energy sales in the recent past — 2.85 percent between 1965 and 1974 — it is clear that "experienced judgments," rather than a simple process of trending, were accorded considerable weight in the City Light forecast.

In fact, Woodfill's forecast was based upon the assumption that certain historical trends would be reversed! The 3.7 percent growth rate was actually a composite of projected growth rates among City Light's three most important classes of customer: industrial, commercial, and residential. Woodfill forecasted discrete annual growth rates of 5.4 percent for the industrial sector, 3.9 percent for the commercial sector, and only 2.6 percent for the residential sector. Taken together these growth rates represented a reversal of historical trends in which the residential sector had exhibited a much higher rate of growth than the industrial sector. Indeed, the past growth rate of energy sales to industrial users was only 1 percent per year, a long way from the forecasted rate of 5.4 percent. City Light was apparently preparing for a major expansion in the industrial use of electrical energy.

It is one thing to forecast an expansion in the industrial use of electricity; it is quite another to provide incentives in the form of a subsidy for such growth. This result was due less to Woodfill's forecast than to City Light's general policy of average cost pricing, which averages the high cost of new thermally generated power with the utility's low cost hydropower, in effect providing a subsidy for all new growth. Further incentives are contained in City Light's special industrial rate. A product of the "city building" era, the industrial rate is characterized by "declining end blocks," i.e., cheaper rates for large users, a holdover from the period of declining cost curves. During a period when the cost of alternative fuels was rapidly rising, the prospect of paying less per unit of electrical energy consumed (while the actual cost to City Light of providing the added energy was rapidly going up) would no doubt be attractive to many large industrial users. Indeed, that was precisely the assumption behind the City Light forecast. According to Woodfill, much of the projected industrial growth would come from heavy energy users, "in which the economic advantages of relatively low-cost energy appear to give weight to expansionary and locational decisions" [*Energy 1990* (Initial Report), Vol. VI, p. 6 - 39].

The high forecast of load growth in the industrial sector would, in connection with a decision to meet future demands with added generation, enable industrial users to take advantage of the incentives embodied in the "declining end blocks" of the industrial rate structure.* A similar situation was evident in the energy sales forecast for the commercial sector. The City Light forecast notes that while the number of commercial customers had not grown in recent years, the commercial load had nevertheless been increasing. The reason for this, according to Woodfill, lay in "modern tendencies toward larger scale operations and buildings," which "consume more energy per unit of working space than their earlier counterparts." [*Energy 1990* (Initial Report), Vol. VI, pp. 6-30, 6-31] These large commercial concerns were also in a position to take advantage of cheap electricity prices since the commercial rate is also based on average cost and

* Industrial consumers pay an "energy charge" of $0.45 per KWH for the first 300 KWH per month and $0.33 per KWH over the first 300 KWH. (In addition, there is a demand charge for industrial customers.) By comparison, the basic residential rate (schedule #22) is composed of "inverted blocks" rather than "declining end blocks," so that most residential users pay energy charges of $0.78 per KWH for the first 480 KWH, $0.99 per KWH for the next 720 KWH, and $1.28 per KWH for any additional units of energy. The rate charged commercial users is also characterized by "declining end blocks," which range from $1.50 per KWH for the smallest users to $0.51 per KWH for the largest. (Electric Rates and Provisions — Seattle City Light.)

includes "declining end blocks" for heavy users . . . .

The growth rates forecasted by Woodfill for these two sectors of City Light customers stand in sharp contrast to another important variable, the rate of employment growth, which, according to the Woodfill forecast, would increase at 2 percent per year — a considerable decline from the past average of 3.6 percent. With electrical energy use by the commercial and industrial sectors forecast to increase at over twice the rate of employment growth, and assuming the ratio of other energy sources to employment remained constant, Seattle's economy would become more energy intensive. During a period of sustained economic growth, a rapid increase in the use of electrical energy might be used to create an infrastructure which in time would create a growing demand for labor. In the context of a more or less settled local economy, however, the rapidly growing use of electrical energy by large users taking advantage of "declining end blocks" might well involve the increasing use of machines in order to cut labor costs. Thus, while business certainly had an interest in the high City Light forecast, the stakes for labor were, if not opposed to those of business, at least more complex than the position taken by their leadership in favor of new generation would seem to indicate.

Unlike the method of "trending" used in the City Light load forecast, Mathematical Sciences Northwest's forecast was based upon the development of an econometric model, which is claimed to have important advantages over the traditional approach. Three of these advantages stand out in particular. Unlike the method of "trending," which assumes that past trends will continue into the future, econometric modeling is able to take account of discontinuities in the various factors which affect energy sales. This is a considerable asset in an environment where rapid changes are taking place, as, for example, in the escalation of the real price of electricity. Econometric modeling is also useful because of its flexibility; alternative forecasts of independent variables can be plugged into the model, or different values can be substituted for them, as new information is gathered. This sort of flexibility is especially useful in policy-making where, for example, the impact of different rate schedules on the growth of demand can be tested. Finally, the requirements for the development of an econometric model — a clear and explicit specification of the relevant variables and the validation of the model through a number of tests — openly reveals its underlying assumptions in a way that "trending," especially when it is modified by informed judgments, does not. Thus, while at first glance econometrics appears to be just the sort of esoteric science which threatens to remove the general public from the process of policy-making, it has a number of qualities which make it a potential ally of democratic decision-making.

Because of the earlier compromise regarding the surplus sale assumption, MSNW did two load forecasts. With City Light's assumption that any surplus power from the nuclear plants could be sold at cost, the econometric model yielded a forecasted annual growth rate of 2.84 percent. With Dr. Shakow's less hopeful assumption that at least some of the surplus nuclear power would have to be sold at less than cost, the forecasted growth rate was a mere 1.52 percent per year. The most important factor in these lower growth rates was the elasticity of the demand for electrical energy. The high cost of nuclear power, about ten times that of hyrdo, would drive up the price of electricity, even when melded with City Light's large hydro base, and the utility's customers would respond by consuming less. This was especially evident in the forecast with the "partial sales assumption," where higher rates, required in order to compensate for lost revenues, dampen demand, resulting in the low growth rate of 1.52 percent. Even with the more optimistic "full assignment of surplus" assumption, however, the growth rate forecasted by MSNW was significantly lower than the City Light forecast of 3.7 percent . . . . *

I said earlier that businesses in Seattle, both in the industrial and commercial sectors, had a stake in the 3.7 percent rate of

---

* The MSNW forecast can be found in Vol. III of the *Energy 1990* Initial Report.

annual growth forecasted by City Light. The logic behind that forecast called for new generation in order to meet the future electrical energy demands of the industrial and commercial sectors, with their respective growth rates of 5.4 percent and 3.9 percent. Moreover, it would be the large energy consumers, the major corporations within these sectors, whose demands would increase fastest as they faced declining cost curves for electricity use because of City Light's average cost pricing and "declining end blocks" of energy. . . .

The MSNW forecast, on the other hand, would seem to have raised serious questions about the advantages of new, high cost nuclear generation. The rising price of electricity, with the addition of costly thermal power, would, according to the consultant, dampen every sector's demand for electrical energy. Large corporations as well as other consumers would reduce their demands as prices rose, and, as a result, new generation would not be necessary. In fact, under the conditions forecasted by MSNW, new generation would not be in anyone's interest, since excess capacity would raise everyone's rates — big business included. The consultant's load forecast, then, would seem to have eliminated corporate Seattle's stake in the City Light forecast and their interest in new and costly thermal generation.

Despite the MSNW forecast, which was published with the rest of the Energy 1990 report at the end of February, 1976, the perspective of corporate Seattle never wavered. Representatives of big business still believed in a higher forecast and continued to support the addition of nuclear power. There are, I think, at least two important reasons for this. First, long-range corporate planning is much easier where a surplus of energy can be taken for granted. Consider the risks to large corporations if City Light is wrong on either the high or the low side of actual demand at some point in the future. A high forecast coupled with unnecessary new generation creates a surplus that must, in the worst case, be sold below cost, which, in turn, raises the rates of all consumers, large corporations included. For such corporations the prospect of increased electricity prices is hardly bothersome. The increased costs, if they are relatively small, can either be absorbed or passed on to consumers. If electricity costs should increase significantly, large corporations would probably be in the best position of anyone, given their resources, to be able to substitute other forms of energy for higher cost electrical power.

On the other hand, a low forecast coupled with a failure to add new generation capacity harbors the potential for an energy shortage. From here there are three possibilities. In the first case additional power would be bought elsewhere, though at high prices, and the results would be similar to those above, i.e., higher electricity costs. In the second case, however, if there were no additional power to be bought, then a genuine shortage would exist and there would be a possibility of temporary shutdowns with a loss of income and perhaps employment. That sort of risk is one for which no large corporation wants to plan. In the third case, City Light would have at least some advance notice of future shortages and would, with approval of the City Council, undertake some sort of mandatory conservation program until new generation could be added to meet demand. This is not the sort of situation in which corporate executives would delight either, since any mandatory measures imposed upon them quite obviously inhibit their freedom of action in the market.

The second reason for the persistence of corporate support for new generation, despite the implications of the MSNW forecast, can be found in the character of possible electrical energy shortages. The private utilities and the aluminum companies are the ones most threatened by the possibility of a Northwest energy shortage. Unless the Bonneville Power Administration (BPA)'s "public preference" clause is rewritten, the low-cost power it has available to sell to private utilities and to its Direct Industrial Service customers (mostly aluminum companies) will rapidly decline. Whether there would be actual curtailments of service to these BPA customers, or whether their rates would rapidly increase with the addition of thermal generation is unclear. In either case, however, many large corporations would have much to lose . . . . These corporations may either operate branches in areas served by private utilities or they may have a stake in rapid regional economic growth. In either case, they would feel the reverberations of an energy shortage suffered by private utilities. For these large regionally-oriented corporations, therefore, a surplus of energy in Seattle would be insurance against the possibility of shortages elsewhere in the Northwest.

The most comprehensive statement of corporate interests in a high load forecast and in new generation can be found in the minority recommendations of the Citizens' Overview Committee, which were published, along with the COC majority recommendations, in the final Energy 1990 report in May of 1976. Of the nine COC members who signed the minority report, six were representatives of the business community . . . . These six individuals constituted, with one exception, the entire business contingent on the COC, and the minority report was, in essence, their creation.

The minority report itself contains three elements which are relevant to the foregoing discussion of the corporate stake in a high forecast and in new generation: a criticism of the MSNW forecast, a plea for City Light cooperation in meeting regional energy needs, and a defense of the market against democratic planning. The report begins with an expression of caution, if not skepticism, toward the MSNW forecast, pointing to the unproven character of econometric modeling in the area of load forecasting. More particularly, the report challenges the forecast of future industrial loads, noting that "forecasters must take account of discrete additions, based on expert information of plans for expansion and improvements by large industrial users." And, in fact, this is not too surprising, since the MSNW forecast differed most sharply from the City Light forecast in estimating future industrial loads . . . . Finally, with respect to the MSNW forecast, the report argues there are much greater risks in a low forecast which would result in shortages. "The costs of brownouts and blackouts, the job losses from shutdown of industry, and the employment lost through failure of new industry to locate here due to inadequate supply are great."

In addition to the possible errors contained in the MSNW forecast, and their consequences, the COC minority based its recommendation for new power generation upon City Light's regional responsibilities. Their report points to the historical cooperation between public and private utilities "in ensuring that the Pacific Northwest region as a whole has had adequate electric energy available to its citizens." It reminds us that City Light purchases 25 percent of its power from the BPA, with the implication that Seattle's municipally owned utility ought to help meet future demands that BPA will no longer be able to supply. According to the minority report, City Light has an obligation to help in the financing of new thermal power plants, which, while necessary to supply regional energy demands, are nevertheless too expensive for the utilities serving the region to construct on their own. Finally, they argue, any surplus power which becomes available to City Light can be sold through the regional network "at the prevailing market price." Selling surplus power to the region is, they claim, "beneficial in keeping rates at the lowest possible level," and, it might be added, in keeping private utilities and aluminum companies supplied with power.

The minority report's recommendation in favor of City Light's participation in the two nuclear power plants is also supported by an appeal to ideological as well as practical considerations. In the first place, it is argued that "delivering electricity desired by the public has been and is the primary responsibility of this utility." And it is through the price mechanism that utilities such as City Light must determine the public's demand for electricity.

> It is contrary to public utility philosophy and operating principles and also contrary to free enterprise philosophy that the amount of energy available should be artificially controlled by placing limits on the appetite of the public.*

---

* This particular appeal to the market in support of the continued increase of supply ignores the collective dimension of electricity as a public good. The COC minority's argument implies that consumers determine the price of electricity through their individual decisions about how much energy to buy. This

According to the minority, City Light should not allow the "new societal environment" to obscure the utility's "traditional responsibilities." The city, in their view, ought to "trust the good judgment of consumers to adjust their purchases" to higher prices, rather than taking the "elitist" approach of "mandatory constraints imposed by a few policymakers to determine how much the public will need."

THE ENERGY QUESTION AND THE SEATTLE PUBLIC

When the COC minority referred to "a 'new age' philosophy" and to "a certain 'elitism' " involved in the reliance upon planning as opposed to the market, they had in mind, perhaps, the environmentalists who had brought the lawsuit in the first place and who formed their most vociferous opposition on the COC. In defending the public's desire to make its choices through the market, however, the COC minority had to overlook strong expressions of public support for energy planning and demand management. For, whenever the active public expressed itself — in the City Light questionnaire, at the public hearings on Energy 1990, in written comments on the Draft EIS, and in the COC majority recommendations — they expressed a marked preference for conservation over nuclear generation.

The City Light questionnaire on Energy 1990 was a remarkable project in several respects. Mailed out in January of 1976, just prior to the publication of the 1990 preliminary report, the questionnaire was sent with the monthly City Light bill to each of the utility's 233,000 residential customers. Of the 12,000 questionnaires which were returned, 6,855 were tabulated. In

view of the matter, however, obscures the fact that if Seattle were to buy surplus power to meet the needs of large users taking advantage of "declining end blocks," the price of electricity to the individual residential user would go up whether he or she used more energy or not. The COC minority's defense of the market was also flawed by their refusal to support even the *study* of long-run incremented cost pricing, which would provide customers with a much more accurate picture of the true costs of supplying additional units of energy.

response to the question, "Do we need more or less energy planning for our future," nearly 80 percent favored more planning at each level of government, while in no case did more than 3 percent prefer less planning. In response to a number of options concerning City Light's possible strategies vis-à-vis the growth rate of electricity use, 52.3 percent felt that City Light should "help try to lessen the demand for electricity," 37 percent felt that it should "strive to supply whatever amount of electric energy is demanded," 32.5 percent were in favor of trying "to increase the use of electricity to save fossil fuels," and only 3.4 percent were of the opinion that City Light should "not make those kinds of decisions." Asked whether City Light should "be permitted to promote conservation," 90.3 percent responded affirmatively and only 3.9 percent negatively. And finally, when asked to rate the relative importance of six different factors in energy planning, 38.2 percent placed the "environment" first, 20.9 percent placed the "local economy" in the top ranking, and 10.4 percent put the "region" in this category . . . .

When City Light and OPP decided upon an Environmental Impact Statement as part of the Energy 1990 study, they committed themselves to a structure of public involvement which included public hearings and a provision for written public comment. The public hearings were scheduled to take place in the middle of March, 1976, a few weeks after the publication of the 1990 study at the end of February. At the time there was a rumor that Wayne Larkin, chairperson of the City Council's Utilities Committee and a friend of Gordon Vickery, had a bet with Michael Hildt, the Council staff member responsible for the 1990 study and a well-known conservationist. Larkin bet that the hearings would attract little public interest, and he lost; the hearings were packed, with oral presentations by interested citizens going on for two days. To add to Larkin's woes, the hearings were packed with critics of new generation. Of the statements published in the final 1990 report, the overwhelming majority expressed either support for conservation as an alternative to new generation or criticism of nuclear power, with only a handful of individuals speaking in favor of nuclear participation.

Those who did support City Light's participation in the two nuclear plants tended to be either business representatives or individuals defending the executive prerogatives of "the experts"....

On the other hand, the opposition to nuclear power seemed to have broadened its social base since the inception of the 1990 study. From the very beginning there were those who opposed nuclear power on account of the safety risks involved. At the hearings a number of individuals, many of them from environmental groups, reiterated these concerns. In the meantime, however, these environmentalists were joined by a growing group of citizens concerned about the costs of nuclear power, which seemed to increase with every new estimate. They provided the sort of measured criticisms that would be most persuasive with Council members searching for some familiar criteria upon which to make a decision....

The extensive public response to the 1990 study was possible in part because of the role of the media in presenting the issues to the public. Nearly 100 newspaper articles were written between the time when City Light made its original request in April, 1975, and the day when the Council made its final decision in July, 1976....

Television and radio stations also devoted a good deal of coverage to Energy 1990. In addition to regular news coverage, interviews with City Light officials were broadcast on radio. And on television there were a number of special features devoted to Energy 1990. One of the more interesting of these appeared on KING-TV's People Power program. Besides discussing the 1990 study and the costs and benefits of future scenarios, the program presented the alternatives of new generation vs. conservation plus solar or wind power, in a new light.

> There you see the options side by side. On the one hand, small-scale technology and personal responsibility for efficient power generation; on the other, centralized power generation that

depends on a corps of highly skilled technologists and technicians.

Recognizing perhaps that conservation would be an acceptable alternative only if the public supported it, the producers of the show ended it with the following appeal:

> Freedom means taking responsibility for your own life. If we don't build the big centralized generating plants, each of us will have to take more responsibility for meeting our energy needs. How much are you willing to take? That's what Seattle City Light and the Seattle City Council need to know.

. . . The constituency which had been developing behind a new approach to energy policy in Seattle was given a further push, and some leadership, when the Citizens' Overview Committee majority recommendations came out at the end of April. The first sentence was to the point: "The Committee recommends that no new additional generation be initiated at this time." The proposal to this effect had been offered by committee member Gene Woodruff. That the recommendation was proposed by Woodruff had some symbolic importance, for he was a nuclear engineer who had argued the virtues of nuclear power at the Council hearings dealing with City Light's original request. The recommendation itself was supported by eighteen of the twenty-seven COC members. Among them were, of course, the environmentalists who had pretty much been opposed to new generation all along. They were joined, however, by the two other groups on the committee which constituted the "swing vote," the academics and those representing various civic organizations in Seattle.

The majority recommendation against new generation was based in part upon a commitment to conservation as an alternative to new power plants. The report noted that "the need for conservation has been repeatedly stated by a wide spectrum of individuals and no one has publicly questioned the necessity for it." Indeed, the COC had unanimously recommended a set of policies aimed at encouraging conservation. The majority, however, went beyond this, arguing that if additional generation were to be included in the city's policy, then there would be no real incentive to conserve. This argument was one of the most remarkable aspects of the entire 1990 process. At the beginning of the 1990 study the aura of uncertainty surrounding Seattle's energy future was, in combination with the inertia of past policies, perhaps the weightiest factor pointing toward new generation. The COC majority, however, was not only willing to accept the risk of future shortages, it was willing to rely on that risk as a necessary motivation to conserve.

The majority's position against new generation was coupled with a number of other recommendations in addition to the conservation proposal. Together, these recommendations amounted to a new energy policy for Seattle, and a new role for City Light. The rate policy adopted by the majority was aimed primarily at managing the demand for electricity in Seattle. Two of its elements, a winter surcharge and a conservation incentive rebate, were aimed directly at reducing demands on the utility. A third, which involved a study of marginal cost pricing, would increase rates considerably to reflect the high cost of supplying power from new generating facilities, and would, in turn, greatly diminish the need for new facilities. Recognizing that such recommendations, in combination with the conservation proposal, constituted a departure from City Light's traditional role, the COC majority affirmed the city's "legal authority to establish, maintain and enforce a program of energy conservation in its service area," and recommended the use of legal principles to achieve "a viable energy policy." Recognizing, too, that the majority was calling for a change from the conventional utility mandate of supplying whatever electricity was demanded, the same business-oriented minority which called for nuclear participation also rejected the COC statement on legal policy.

CONSERVATION

One of the more intriguing aspects of Energy 1990 was the way in which the meaning of "conservation" was transformed, and its appeal as an alternative to more generating facilities increasingly broadened. When the 1990 study began, the notion of conservation was mainly confined to City Light's "Kill-a-Watt" program. That program was begun in 1973 during the oil embargo and its theme was what City Light called "energy ethics." It was a program of voluntary curtailment in which City Light urged its customers to turn off their lights, turn down their heat, and develop a new "energy awareness." It was good public relations, and perhaps effective over the short term, but it was not a policy the Council would be willing to count on as a long-run solution to the city's energy problem . . . .

In the course of becoming a viable alternative, the meaning of conservation had changed. The appeal to a new "energy ethics, living lightly," was withdrawn and in its place was substituted a collection of cost-effective conservation measures. Home insulation would save far more energy than turning off the lights, and policy-makers would not have to rely on voluntary self-discipline, but rather on the more reliable motives of self-interest; for as OPP had demonstrated, an investment in insulation would bring a greater return than money left in the bank. It was now argued, and in fact held to be a virtue, that conservation would mean no change in Seattle's "life style."

If the Council was going to decide in favor of an aggressive conservation program as opposed to new generation facilities, it would need to know, in addition to how much energy could be saved through a conservation program, whether or not the public would support it. This was essential because an effective conservation program would require some mandatory measures which most certainly would meet with resistance in some quarters of the public mind. It was, in this connection, significant that much of the impulse for conservation came from the COC rather than from the City Council. A program which included a number of stiff regulations, such as meeting heat loss standards in order to convert to electric heating, would stand a much better chance of winning public acceptance if it were initiated by citizens themselves rather than by an agency of city government. The COC recommendation formed the apex of public support which included below it a contingent of civic activists who had spoken at the public hearings and a wider base of support that was to be found in the overwhelming approval of conservation by those responding to the City Light questionnaire.

Although public support for conservation was widespread, it was supported for a number of different reasons, not all of which had to do with "cost-effectiveness." To many, of course, it was appealing simply because it was comparatively cheap. According to OPP's calculations, it would cost about six times more to generate a new KWH of electrical energy than to save one. For others, however, conservation was appealing because it was an environmentalist strategy. By saving energy, the need for new power plants of any kind could be forestalled. As it became more and more apparent that conservation could save enough energy to meet future needs, many ordinary Seattle citizens, already committed to some degree of environmentalism, joined the "extremists" in advocating conservation as an alternative to the nuclear plants. There was developing, thus, an alliance in support of conservation between many citizens who thought mainly in terms of economic costs on the one hand and those who thought in terms of more qualitative costs on the other.

For many environmentalists, of course, conservation was more than a practical solution to Seattle's energy problem; it was a morally praiseworthy alternative to present wastefulness. They hoped, perhaps, to generate a more deeply committed "energy ethics," beyond anything contemplated by the authors of the "Kill-a-Watt" campaign, for the reason that it *would* mean a new "life style." The "environmental extremists," as their growth-minded opponents called them, were not, however, the only ones who saw the conservation alternative in moral terms. Many civic organizations and activists — the League of Women Voters, a number of community councils, the chairperson of the Seattle 2000 Commission's energy committee, etc. — came to regard conservation in what could also be called moral terms.

These groups and individuals, infected by civic pride, wanted to make Seattle into a model of conservation to which the rest of the country could turn for a solution to the energy crisis. They would reclaim for Seattle the position of national leadership that City Light had earlier won for it in the heyday of public power. If these citizens had their way the Council would adopt Scenario #5, the 1990 report's "steady state" version of the conservation ideal, and Seattle would become "a city on a hill."

Many of the opponents of conservation, as an *alternative* to nuclear power, also regarded the issue from a moral point of view. The point of contention, especially within the COC, was the morality of mandatory conservation. The most critical view of the conservation alternative was to be found not so much in the COC minority report, where criticism of mandatory conservation takes the indirect route of praising "voluntary conservation," as in the dissenting statements of two COC members who voted with the minority. Interestingly, neither was a representative of business. One of them was Brian Doherty, secretary of the Roofers and Waterproofers Local #54. His comments, filled with suspicion of middle-class Seattle, suggest that conservation is the ideology of the status quo. Energy, he says, is "fluid capital," which is contrasted with conservation which Doherty calls "capital frozen." "Frozen to an ideology of conservation — good when we are *all* warm and comfortable, not so good when there are other, more immediate needs." Conservation, it must have seemed to him, was an obstacle to social justice, the embodiment of middle-class complacency, while energy, on the other hand, held the promise of "change" and "progress," and, of course, the immediate prospect of more jobs.

THE SUPERINTENDENT'S RECOMMENDATION: MANAGERIAL PREROGATIVE, ORGANIZATIONAL INTEREST, AND THE POLITICS OF REGIONAL ENERGY PLANNING

The COC recommendation against participation in the nuclear plants, coupled with the strong public support for conservation in the City Light poll, at the public hearings, and in the written response to the 1990 report, seemed to be on the verge of turning the city's energy policy in a new direction. Then, on May 21, 1976, came Superintendent Vickery's recommendation in favor of a host of new generation facilities: 5 percent participation in the nuclear plants (as opposed to the original request of 10 percent), a dam on Copper Creek, the raising of Ross Dam, and two coal-fired generators. A conservation program was also included, but its importance paled against the background of Vickery's request for more power. The COC majority was angry, the 1990 consultant was critical, and the City Light economist who prepared the utility's original forecast, Doug Woodfill, was so disenchanted that he publicly resigned at the Council hearings, charging Vickery with making a "sham" of public involvement. Vickery himself, however, had other constituencies besides these to consider.

In response to a question concerning the character of his recommendation, Vickery replied, "Sure it's political in some places, that's what this whole thing's about." It was a frank and perfectly accurate reply. The recommendation contained, first of all, a defense of the superintendent's prerogative. Vickery argued that the utility planner, unlike the "economist" (i.e., Dr. Shakow), "must accommodate all reasonable eventualities on a sound economic basis. . . . A prudent facilities planning program," he went on, "must look beyond the forecast and be designed for flexibility and to accommodate uncertainty. . . ." With these words Vickery attempted to recreate the atmosphere of unpredictability which surrounded the origin of Energy 1990 and within which the consultant's load forecast would lose some of its persuasive force, giving way to the claims of experienced judgment and executive prerogative. Translated into quantitative terms, that prerogative amounted to a 68MW [megawatts] "general contingency planning reserve," plus, it could be argued, another 145MW as a "statistical confidence factor" (reflecting Vickery's lack of faith in the MSNW model), both of which were added onto the consultant's forecast.

If Vickery once thought himself accountable to the COC, his recommendation indicated that he no longer did so. In fact, sometime later Vickery complained that *they* had abandoned him, providing their advice to the City Council rather than to City Light. In any case, he ignored the 1990 study (some claimed he had not even read it), and brought in the veterans at City Light to do the superintendent's "revised forecast." Despite the political disadvantages which would appear later, this strategy had two immediate benefits. In the first place, Vickery could count on a forecast that would be revised upwards, for reasons of interest and outlook that were discussed earlier. And secondly, the assignment of this responsibility to the old guard would bring an important part of Vickery's organization back "into the fold," at the same time providing him with defenders to help answer the criticism that would no doubt be forthcoming. Among the aspects of the "revised forecast" which reflected the orientation of the old guard was the discounting of energy savings produced by City Light's Kill-a-Watt program. The 60MW annual load reduction that was attributable to the utility's voluntary conservation program would be reduced to 30 MW by 1990, according to the new forecast. It was a revision which, in the view of those responsible for power generation, returned the utility's priorities to their proper place.

Besides the 145MW and 68MW added to the MSNW forecast as a "statistical confidence factor" and a "general contingency planning reserve," respectively, Vickery's revised forecast included 90MW of "discrete industrial load additions." The political significance of these additions should not have escaped those who followed the 1990 process, for it had already been revealed that Vickery was serving on the Board of Trustees of the Seattle Chamber of Commerce, and that City Light was a member of the Downtown Development Association. To arrive at the figure of 90MW for "industrial additions," Vickery had the Lighting Department do a survey of nineteen large industrial customers, asking about their plans for possible electrical conversions or additions to existing plants. From the total of

230MW, which according to one COC member represented the additional load if every conceivable conversion were undertaken, Vickery settled on the figure of 90MW for which he argued there was "adequate evidence available," though he later called it "proprietary information" and refused to make it available to the COC....

Besides his constituency within the City Light organization and among the utility's industrial customers, Vickery also had a regional clientele which included other utility executives, BPA's industrial customers, and those organizations with a stake in a fast pace of economic growth within the region — all of whom shared fears of a future power shortatge. Vickery had opened up a Pandora's box by permitting an independent load forecast, which would eventually threaten the traditional prerogatives of utility executives interested in high forecasts and plant expansion. And the notion that Seattle had finished its days of "city building," wherein City Light provided a surplus of cheap power to attract industry to the area, did not sit well with those in eastern Washington who still had their cities yet to build. If Vickery and City Light were going to play a leading role in regional energy planning, then support from these increasingly suspicious constituencies would have to be won. Vickery's recommendation for new generating facilities, and in particular his request that City Light participate in financing the nuclear plants with other utilities of the region, went some distance toward alleviating this suspicion, and his later efforts to find buyers for City Light's surplus power went the rest of the way.

The Mayor, the Newspapers, and the City Council Vote Against Nuclear Participation

Shortly after Vickery made his recommendation, Mayor Uhlman made his. Uhlman supported the superintendent's request for nuclear participation, provided there was reasonable assurance that any surplus power could be sold at full cost until City Light needed it. The mayor was steering a course between the superintendent and the COC's recommendations, and, more important, between his two opponents for Governor — environmentalist Marvin Durning and nuclear power proponent Dixy Lee Ray. *The Weekly* [June 2, 1976] called it a "nondecision," pointing out that if the Council were to vote against him "Uhlman can seize the initiative and say that he has not been 'assured' enough by industrial users and therefore he too opts for nonparticipation."

. . . Following Uhlman's recommendation, Vickery seized the initiative by lining up potential buyers for the surplus power, hoping the mollify some of his critics. . . . As the deadline for the Council's decision approached, Vickery informed the Council members that negotiations with nineteen major Northwest companies concerning the sale of surplus power were going well, although binding contracts were not expected by July 12, the day of the vote. Shortly thereafter, Vickery gave to the City Council two letters of intent from potential surplus buyers — one from Pacific Power and Light of Portland, and one from a group of industrial companies whose BPA allocation was to be cut in 1983. The *Times* was pleased, claiming that Vickery's letters of intent had "destroyed his critics" and that City Light now had a "'can't lose' nuclear power chance" [June 28, 1976]. . . .

In addition to winning the editorial endorsement of Seattle's two major newspapers, Vickery's request for nuclear power drew support from the city's most powerful business and labor organizations. Individuals from these organizations continued to regard nuclear power as a prerequisite for further economic growth, despite the 1990 study's effort to separate the two issues. Among the business organizations supporting Vickery were the Seattle chapter of the National Electrical Contractors Association, the Civic Builders Committee, Puget Power, the Chamber of Commerce, the Downtown Development Association, and the Port of Seattle. Labor support for nuclear participation came from the Inside Electrical Workers Union and the Building Trades Council among other organizations. By most standards, it was an awesome coalition. . . .

The Citizens' Overview Committee, which had proven to be a thorn in Vickery's side from the beginning, was allowed a front row seat during the Council hearings on the superintendent's recommendation. They had already criticized Vickery's hiring of more consultants to help prepare his recommendation, and when it came out, they lashed into it with relish. Dr. Shakow pointed out that he had already added 60MW of industrial additions to his forecast and saw no reason for another 90. And one COC member pointed out that "allowing industries that additional 90MW of energy would be tantamount to subsidizing their increased electrical usage with Seattle's 5 percent, $100 million to $125 million, 89MW nuclear share." Other COC representatives criticized Vickery for violating the 1990 process by bringing in new information at the last minute, and Council member John Miller proceeded to ask for written justifications of City Light's new figures. And, finally, when Vickery came in later with contracts for the sale of surplus power, the lawyers on the COC pointed out the high risks involved; the first call-back of power would require eight years' advance notice, and Seattle alone would bear the financial burden if the nuclear plants were shut down for safety reasons or for improvements. Vickery's recommendation had won powerful supporters, but in light of the COC's sustained criticism, *it* now began to appear as the alternative fraught with uncertainty.

Of course reasoned argument alone, cut off from any constituency, would not be persuasive with the Council. The conservation alternative, however, had been winning supporters all along. Together, they formed a classic progressive coalition — environmentalists, academics, community councils, the League of Woman Voters, People Power, Metrocenter, and the Muncipal League — the sort of middle-class groups that were coming to exercise more and more power in this middle-class city. People Power, in particular, played an important role in coordinating the allies of conservation, giving advice to interested citizens as to which Council members were undecided and what sort of arguments would be most persuasive with them. The biggest issue in

Seattle in five or ten years shaped up as a battle between "the interests" and the city's well coordinated voluntary associations.

One further legacy of public power, beyond the public's high expectations of City Light, was the fact that Seattle's energy policy had been publicly debated for over a year and was going to be decided by the City Council rather than the Puget Power Board of Directors. The members of the City Council were by now considerably more informed and confident in dealing with the questions of energy policy, and, while they had been interested spectators throughout most of the 1990 process, they now gathered in the reins of authority. As one Council member said just prior to the final decision, "The electrical growth rate will be what five votes says it is." This comment not only expressed the Council's independence vis-a-vis the mayor and the superintendent, it also acknowledged the political nature of the upcoming decision, a fact which had been temporarily obscured by those who had earlier hoped that an independent, objective forecast would settle the issue.

While it could be taken for granted that the City Council would decide the issue of nuclear participation, it was also widely believed, from the very beginning, that the Council would approve City Light's request to buy into the nuclear plants. David Brewster [of *the Weekly*] had written back in October that the Council would "undoubtedly" vote for nuclear participation; and despite all that had happened since then, Duff Wilson [of the *Argus*], who was probably the most sensitive observer of the 1990 process, still believed in June that a number of factors continued to point "toward a Council majority voting in favor of new generation." Among those factors Wilson included: the role of an assured surplus in attracting industry to Seattle, creating new jobs, and expanding the city's tax base; empathy with City Light executives who were being subjected to a constant barrage of criticism; and the need for financial support on the part of those Council members who were running for mayor [the *Argus,* June 18, 1976].

In spite of these factors, however, the Council voted 6 to 3 against participation in the nuclear plants. . . . In explaining their decision, several Council members voting with the majority wanted to emphasize that theirs was not a vote against growth, and only Sam Smith mentioned the problems of safety in connection with the nuclear plants. The principal justifications given were, rather, the lack of a demonstrated need for more energy, the high cost of nuclear power, and the effect additional generation would have in undermining the conservation program which the Council had just adopted.

Although by the time of the Council's final decision the question of cost had become paramount, it was not cost in general that produced the 6 to 3 vote against participation in the nuclear plants. The city's large corporations, after all, were perfectly willing to pay bigger utility bills in order to have a guaranteed surplus of electrical energy. It was, rather, the increased costs to residential users — whether they used more electricity or not — that prompted the vote against nuclear power. In this middle-class city, where there is such an extraordinary percentage of homeowners, it is oftentimes neither business, nor labor, nor environmentalists, but neighborhoods which form the City Council's natural constituency. This tendency was greatly accentuated in the 1990 decision because City Light's rate schedule distributes the costs of electricity unevenly among industrial, commercial, and residential classes of customers. Thus, the Council's vote can be seen in part as an effort to protect the city's residential consumers from the high cost of nuclear power purchased in order to provide big businesses with a reservoir of surplus power and Superintendent Vickery with a larger role in regional energy negotiations.

CONCLUSION

One of the difficulties involved in writing about a long-term decision-making process such as Energy 1990 is that of combining a narrative description of events with a schematic treatment of their underlying political themes. Because the history of Energy 1990 is not readily accessible, at least in any one published place, I have had to devote a considerable portion of the paper to the telling of a story. What I want to do in this conclusion, therefore, is to collect together some of the themes of the study in a very abbreviated and schematic way.

The first theme I want to mention is City Light's relation to the Seattle public. In the paper I suggested that one legacy of public power in Seattle has been the public's high expectation of, and identification with, its municipally owned utility. One important result of this relationship was, I believe, the willingness of so many citizens to grant City Light new powers in order to carry out a program of demand management. Without this willingness, the City Council could not have chosen the conservation alternative in lieu of new generation facilities. A second theme that belongs under this heading is the effect of rising cost curves in increasing consumer activism among a public accustomed to low electricity rates. Without this increasing public concern over higher electricity prices, and the threat it posed to the legitimacy of the Vickery regime, the environmentalist critics of City Light policy would have had to fight a lonely and, doubtless, losing battle for a new energy policy.

A second set of themes discussed in the paper centers around the progressive character of the 1990 process and a few observations concerning Seattle's current brand of progressivism in general. I take two of the principal features of progressivism to be a reliance upon technocratic rationality, on the one had, and a commitment to citizen participation, on the other. In hoping to resolve Seattle's energy problem by resorting to an "independent, objective" load forecast, the city's policy-makers expressed their faith in the former. Likewise, the cost-benefit framework established by OPP, and, in some sense, accepted by the City Council, was another expression of faith in the power of instrumental rationality. Although the methods employed in developing the load forecast and in evaluating the cost effectiveness of conservation measures were not readily accessible to the general public, they nevertheless proved, in this case at least, to be allies of accountability, deflating the claims of managerial prerogative and reducing the impact of some of the exaggerated consequences of non-generation predicted by the advocates of nuclear power. On the other hand, however, by relying so heavily upon what was hoped to be an "objective" analysis of the city's future energy needs, Seattle's policy-makers too often avoided a public discussion of what the *purposes* of its energy policy ought to be. As a consequence, the issue of growth, or better yet, what kinds of growth ought to be encouraged, went undiscussed, except in the case where advocates of "progress" took the virtues of any sort of economic growth for granted.

The promise held out by proponents of "citizen participation" is not often realized in the determination of issues as important as those involved in Energy 1990. There were, however, a number of factors which contributed to the effectiveness of citizen participation in the 1990 process: those selected to serve on the Selection and Overview Committees had, in most instances, both some expertise and a constituency; they were involved early on and at key points in the process; they had at their disposal staff support from OPP, City Light, and the City Council; and their role was supplemented by other avenues of public involvement through which large numbers of citizens could express their views. Thanks to these circumstances, the COC was able to protect the autonomy of the consultant, to change the shape of the study, to develop a viable conservation alternative, and to forcefully challenge the recommendations of the superintendent. This was a remarkable set of achievements — by any standard of democratic decision-making.

Most of the wider public response to Energy 1990, beyond the role of the COC, was anchored in Seattle's numerous and well-organized voluntary associations. They form the nerves of what I have called the City Council's residential constituency. And, if the role of these civic groups (community councils, People Power, etc.) in the Energy 1990 process is at all indicative of their importance in Seattle's politics, then those theories which minimize the importance of voluntary associations in local politics are of little use in understanding what goes on in this city. These are the bastions of progressive, middle-class politics, and while they did not pay a great deal of attention to the impact of energy decisions upon the poor (nor did anyone else for that matter),* neither did they, as the revisionist interpretation of progressivism would seem to suggest, serve to advance the interests of corporate power.

A third focus of this paper has been the organization of City Light. Among other things, I have tried to describe the nature and organizational basis for the internal conflicts which continue to disturb our municipally owned utility. In particular, I emphasized the importance of new power generation facilities for many of the organizational sub-units within City Light, and the significance of perspectives shaped during the time when City Light was developing its relatively cheap base of hydroelectric power. In addition to this internal focus, I have also tried to say something about City Light's external clientele, especially among its large industrial customers and among other utilities within the region. For the latter, and particularly for the private utilities which operate in the Northwest, the Energy 1990 process posed a serious threat, calling into question utility-influenced forecasts and attitudes toward conservation. Finally, these internal and external constraints formed the context in which I attempted to explain Superintendent Vickery's recommendation for additional generation and his subsequent attempts to line up buyers for Seattle's surplus power.

The fourth, and probably most ambitious, theme of the paper is to be found in the section on the political economy of load forecasting. Taken by themselves, load forecasts for the city's future consumption of electrical energy have little meaning. When broken down by sector and placed in the context of City Light's rate structure, however, it is possible to understand the economic and political significance of these forecasts for various interests

* The Energy 1990 study devoted only a few pages to the question of the "effects of rising electricity prices on low-income households." See *Energy 1990* (Initial Report), Vol. 1, pp. 2-22 to 2-24.

in the city. In this regard, I have tried to demonstrate what was at stake in the growth rates forecasted by City Light and MSNW, and to show how rapidly rising cost curves and the possibility of energy shortages raise new questions about the distribution of risks to City Light's customers. The conclusions of this section are, even more than in the others, preliminary in nature. More work needs to be done, in particular on: (1) corporate interests in new generation; (2) the question of labor's interest in a more energy intensive economy; (3) the character of electricity as a semi-public good; and (4) the impact of rising electricity prices on the poor.

Another major theme, finally, has been the sociocultural bases of support for conservation in Seattle. Here, I have tried to describe how conservation, as an alternative to nuclear power, was developed by the COC non-generation subcommittee and the Office of Policy Planning, and supported by many of the civic groups mentioned above. In addition, there was a too-brief discussion of the various cultural bases of that support which ranged from methodical cost calculation to environmentalism to civic pride. I also noted the hostility to conservation on the part of business, the autonomy of which would be threatened by mandatory measures, and labor, whose representative on the COC regarded conservation as an obstacle to social justice. This last claims deserves further consideration, for it is not at all clear that the construction of new generation facilities would provide more jobs than a thorough-going conservation program. If, in fact, conservation actually created more jobs than the construction of nuclear plants, then support for Seattle's Energy 1990 as a solution to the region's energy future could be broadened to include at least some segments of organized labor, which, together with conservation's middle-class appeal, would make a formidable coalition.

Bonneville

E. KIMBARK MacCOLL

This excerpt is from The Growth of a City: Power and Politics in Portland, Oregon, 1915 to 1950, *the second of a projected three volume history of Portland. Volume 1,* The Shaping of a City, *covered the period from 1885 to 1915 and is now being revised for a second printing. Volume 3,* Destruction and Renewal, Business and Politics in Portland, Oregon 1950-1980, *is scheduled for publication in 1984. Kim MacColl is a historian, teacher and publisher. He lives in Portland.*

The Bonneville and the Grand Coulee, the first federal dams on the main stream of the Columbia River, became the cornerstones for the world's largest hydroelectric power system, which today includes 29 major federal dams and 124 other federal and non-federal hydroelectric projects. Of the nation's total hydroelectric potential, the Pacific Northwest today possesses more than 40 percent.

During the early months of 1934, few people in either Washington, D.C., or the Northwest foresaw the possibilities of such expansive growth. As one observer has noted, "No river in history has undergone so complete a metamorphosis in such a short period of time." Both Bonneville and Grand Coulee were "crash programs" undertaken in the early days of the New Deal to provide jobs to the unemployed and in the process to help stimulate the nation's sagging economy. As General Martin's memorandum indicated, improvement of navigation was the primary function to be served by Bonneville Dam. Power generation was strictly a secondary consideration. But regardless of how the dam's purposes were perceived, few could argue with

The Oregon Journal's comment that "for better or for worse, Portland is embarked on a great new adventure." Some of the local realtors felt the same way. One firm, but the name of Keasey, Hurley and Keady, began buying up large chunks of land adjacent to the dam site. Between October 1933 and March 1934, property values increased from $30 an acre to between $250 and $500 an acre. The federal government was forced to move in quickly and to condemn much of the land on both sides of the dam site. The boom subsided as quickly as it had arisen.

Apart from giving Oregonians a psychological uplift, the proposed construction of Bonneville Dam had statewide political implications. It sharpened the debate between the private and public power forces and created severe fragmentation within both the Republican and Democratic parties as the 1934 gubernatorial primaries approached. More than any other issue, strong differences of opinion over public power prevented the Democratic Party from creating the type of coalition that would have allowed it to challenge effectively the Republican Party's traditional dominance of the state legislature. During the New Deal years, Oregon remained essentially a Republican state despite the fact that Roosevelt carried the state twice and despite the anomalous elections of Independent Julius L. Meier and Democrat Charles H. Martin as governors. Martin was to be elected in November 1934 after a free-for-all campaign that left national political observers scratching their heads in disbelief.

When Julius Meier announced that he would not seek reelection, "Republican Party politics became a tangled skein."[*] Five candidates entered the Republican primary, including State Treasurer Rufus Holman, a long-time public power advocate. Representative Martin was induced to announce his Democratic candidacy by both Oswald West and President Roosevelt, who apparently did not realize Martin's real views on public power. But even if he had, there was little

*Robert Earl Burton, "A History of the Democratic Party in Oregon, 1900-1956," Ph. D. dissertation (Eugene: University of Oregon, 1969), 139.

he could do about the matter. Roosevelt was forced to work through the existing state party organization that was largely controlled by West who was the Democratic National Committeeman. As a paid lobbyist for Pacific Power & Light, West was obviously not sympathetic to public power development.

Martin, in fact, was already on record as opposed to FDR's "yardstick principle." In the fall of 1933, after the Bonneville Dam was authorized, Martin had told the Portland Realty board: "The power which the government will develop at Bonneville is not intended to force down the rates of existing power companies. This power is intended for the great chemical and metallurgical reduction plants whose first consideration is cheap power and an inexhaustible supply." This was the position, essentially, that both the Portland Chamber of Commerce and the private utilities were to maintain until after the passage of the Bonneville Power Administration Act in 1937.

Martin's position on the future distribution of federal power split the ranks of the Democratic Party. The public power faction in turn became divided over personality issues so that Martin was able to secure the nomination with 58 percent of the vote. The Republicans were equally fragmented over public power and personality questions. As a result, the most conservative of the candidates, Joe Dunne, won the nomination with only 30 percent of the vote. With neither of the major gubernatorial candidates favoring public power development, a third candidate emerged to secure nomination as an Independent. He was state senator Peter Zimmerman from Yamhill County, an old-time progressive Republican of the George Joseph–Julius Meier faction who was often accused of being a socialist.

The election results were hardly conclusive as a measure of public power's popularity. Martin won with only 39 percent of the vote cast. Zimmerman came in second with 32 percent and Dunne wound up third with 29 percent. Martin had the obvious advantage of name familiarity. Both he and Dunne had opposed an Oregon Grange initiative calling for the creation of an elective state commission to finance, transmit and distribute power. The initiative lost by only 14,765 votes and major credit was given to the expensive campaign waged against the measure by the private utilities. Paul McKee's presence at Pacific Power & Light was already being felt. This was to be the first of many successful campaigns that he was to fight against the "initiative" of the public power advocates.

A brief mention of Oswald West's activities is in order at this point. To the historian who fondly remembers West as the crusading, progressive, consumer-oriented governor of Oregon from 1911 to 1915, West's subsequent career between the two world wars has overtones of sadness and disappointment. He was not a man of any inherited means or marketable professional skills by which he could support his family. When he was offered the position as a paid lobbyist for the private utilities, he was at least assured a liveable income. From the utilities' vantage point, the hiring of West was a smart move. As a prominent Democrat and national committeeman, West would obviously prove useful. And indeed he did, but with the consequence that his political tactics helped to destroy the Democratic Party in Oregon. Increasingly, he opposed all liberal and progressive measures that were associated with the New Deal. And when Martin failed to win renomination in 1938, West offered little help to the party's more liberal candidate. In fact, Republican Charles Sprague, who became governor in 1938, was to prove far more sympathetic to Roosevelt's public power program than either Martin or West had ever been.

When President Roosevelt steamed into Portland's harbor aboard the *U.S.S. Houston* on August 4, 1934, he must have been aware that he was entering a political hornet's nest. However, he exhibited no visible concern for either the intra-party feud or candidate Martin's negative views on public power. The city was just recovering from the worst waterfront strike in its history and most everyone the President met seemed to be both exhausted and relieved.

After a short parade through downtown Portland, the President and motorcade proceeded to Bonneville by way of the Columbia River Scenic Highway. A special train transported over 1200 people to join the thousands who had arrived earlier by car. In company with outgoing Governor Meier and candidate Martin, Mr. Roosevelt dedicated the site for the new Bonneville Dam. In his brief remarks, the President emphasized what the dam would do for Western Oregon and particularly Portland. It was certain to lead to a "vastly increased population." Portland was the only large city on the main stem of the Columbia. It could grow so large that it might become "unhealthy" and such growth would be at "the expense of smaller communities." Declared Mr. Roosevelt, Portland "could become a huge manufacturing center close to the source of power, a vast city of whirling machinery." Or it might become a center for decentralized regional growth. It was obvious that the President favored the latter development.

President Roosevelt was deeply committed to the concept of regional planning. Earlier in the year, he had encouraged the formation of the Pacific Northwest Regional Planning Commission as an offshoot of the National Resources Committee. A local office had already been established with Marshall Dana as the commission chairman and Roy F. Bessey as the staff director. Also included on the commission were prominent Spokane attorney Benjamin Kizer and City Commissioner Ormand R. Bean. The group's primary purpose was to examine some methods by which existing governmental bodies might cooperate more closely around common interests. The future use and distribution of Columbia River power drew much of their attention. The need to consider regional solutions was already in the minds of many officials of the Roosevelt administration as well as in the thoughts of a few political leaders like Idaho's Senator James Pope. Four months after Mr. Roosevelt's visit, Senator Pope was to introduce the first proposal for a Columbia Valley

Authority (CVA), patterned upon the Tennessee Valley
Authority (TVA) established by Congress in March 1933. The
TVA was, in the President's words, "a corporation clothed with
the power of government, but possessed with the flexibility and
initiative of a private enterprise." Its aim was the unified development of the Tennessee River system by a single, all-purpose
program.

The notion of a CVA type development for the Pacific Northwest was anathema not only to the private utilities but to Oregon's congressional delegation, with the exception of Walter
Pierce. For many Portland business and utility leaders, Mr.
Roosevelt's mentioning of Portland as a future "huge manufacturing center" was ominous enough. But the thought of a
government corporation assuming control over the marketing of
federally generated power was nothing short of socialism. The
CVA concept was to reappear on and off for 20 years but nothing
ever came of it. Oregonians could not conceive of the kinds of
power demands and shortages that were to occur 40 years later,
creating crises that would require a regionally unified program of
power distribution and marketing. In fact, the early critics of the
dam construction program referred to Bonneville as "a dam of
doubt." Where would this vast amount of hydroelectricity ever
be sold, it was asked. "Generators surely would rust, spillways
would crumble, wires never would be energized. The dams even
were compared in obsolescence with the Pyramids of Egypt."
The Portland opponents of the BPA act in 1937 were to charge
that the Northwest was already "choked up with power now."
Why add turbines which would be useless? Naturally, the private
utilities egged on these warnings that the government had erected
costly tombstones across the surging Columbia.

THE EVOLUTION OF THE BPA

Despite fragmented opposition to the dam's erection and
some apprehension it created in the minds of a few staid Portlanders who were concerned about its impact on the natural
environment, the building activity that picked up momentum

early in 1935 drew wide support from Oregonians generally. Particularly appealing was the fact that the dam was employing over 5000 workers in all of the interrelated efforts that went into its construction and equipage. One news release noted that the project was expected to provide 130,777 man-months of employment.

Following these developments closely was the Portland Chamber of Commerce. The chamber leadership appointed a blue ribbon Bonneville Committee composed of: Amedee Smith, former county commissioner and associate of C.F. Swigert in the Willamette Iron and Steel Company, as chairman; R.B. Wilcox of the Wilcox Investment Company and Ladd & Tilton fame, as vice chairman; Henry F. Cabell, grandson of Henry Failing and large investor in PGE; Franklin T. Griffith; Philip L. Jackson, publisher of *The Oregon Journal*; William F. Woodward, prominent Portland businessman and the only member to favor public power; and C.C. Chapman, editor of the *Oregon Voter*. The chamber's primary interest in early 1935 was to search out and identify specific plots of public land which might be available for industrial sites that could take advantage of the future supply of Bonneville power. Named to head the investigation was local attorney George L. Rauch.

Rauch was a prominent member of the Portland business community. He was known for his energy, civic work and integrity. His report that was issued in October 1935 must have surprised some of his chamber colleagues. In the light of recent history, the document was prophetic to say the least. After reviewing various options available to the city, Rauch noted that:

. . . the City has, as now constituted, the right and power . . . by eminent domain or otherwise, to secure electrical power to sell to manufacturing institutions. Perhaps with the same expenditures, the City of Portland could purchase the power facilities of Bonneville, to be distributed directly to industries upon terms sufficiently favorable to secure their location at Portland.

In essence, Rauch told his chamber friends that the city and the chamber should be more concerned with purchasing power rights than with purchasing industrial sites. Certainly either the dock commission or the Port of Portland could acquire property on which to locate future industries that would require the use of Bonneville power. But for the same kind of investment the city could probably purchase a portion of either the facilities or the power output on a long-term contract. In other words, future power supply was more important than land. The implications of Rauch's recommendation did not sit well with the chamber's Bonneville Committee. Such an action, on the city's part, would have put Portland in the municipal power business, if only initially for industrial distribution purposes. Franklin Griffith could well imagine the long-term consequences of such a step. In the fall of 1935, the city council was already debating the desirability of acquiring the Northwestern Electric Company upon the expiration of its franchise in 1937.

In one respect, Rauch was way ahead of his time. Few people among the Portland business community in 1937 could imagine the day when a shortage of power and its high cost would threaten the industrial development of the Portland metropolitan region. In another respect, however, Rauch was no more farsighted than his chamber colleagues. His recommendations were strictly local in nature. Even Rauch did not understand the need for long-term planning on a regional basis as advocated by the Pacific Northwest Regional Planning Commission. But then, of course, in 1935, little support existed anywhere in the Pacific Northwest for a regional electric power grid system.

A month before attorney Rauch delivered his report to the chamber, Commissioner Ralph C. Clyde presented his proposal to the city council to submit to the voters "the question of the acquisition of the Northwestern Electric Company's system." In his covering letter, Clyde wrote:

While we are all rejoicing in the fact that the Bonneville Power development has become a reality, in fact is nearing completion, it is the desire of your Commissioner of Public Utilities to again call to the attention of the Council that if the City of Portland is to reap any real benefit from this development, it must immediately take the necessary steps to provide the means of transmitting this electrical energy to the homes, merchants and manufacturers of our city.

Clyde restated many of the same arguments that he had made in January 1931, that is: (1) Over 2000 other American cities were successfully generating and/or distributing their own electric energy; (2) Eugene and Tacoma had the lowest light and power rates in the Northwest; and (3), once the bonds on a municipally-owned system are paid off, the rates are greatly reduced.

On the other hand, it is the policy of all private power companies never to reduce their bonded indebtedness and they must therefore charge rates sufficiently high to not only meet their expenses of operation but to pay interest on their bonds, dividends on their preferred and common stock as well. This calls for a higher rate structure on the private-owned system than on the municipally-owned one.

Clyde questioned why the federal government would spend $40 million to build a federal power project for the benefit of the private power companies. "If the people of Portland are to benefit directly from this development then it is absolutely necessary that a publicly-owned distribution system be provided." With the franchise of the Northwestern Electric Company due to expire on October 22, 1937, Clyde wanted the voters to be given their rightful opportunity "to determine whether they desire the City to exercise its option to acquire the facilities." Clyde recommended that the issue be submitted at the May 1936 primary.

During the first week of December 1935, the city council debated the merits of Clyde's proposal. The Chamber of Commerce submitted a lengthy statement to Mayor Joseph K. Carson. It requested "full and public discussion" of the issue; the total cost of the acquisition and the amount of rate reduction to offset loss or disturbance of taxes. "The City Council must exert every effort to have the true facts of our [the chamber's] position presented and the false and misleading statements that are made at this time by the advocates of a move to put the city in the municipal power business discounted." The chamber concluded that a public hearing should "avoid creating the impression . . .

that Portland is at a disadvantage when compared with other cities.''

Mayor Carson was not a supporter of Clyde's proposal. He was a close associate of Oswald West's and had won election as mayor in 1933 while he was secretary of the State Democratic Committee. Like his friend, Governor Martin, Carson had wanted Bonneville Dam primarily as a source of power for new industry. He was not in sympathy with any move to municipalize a private power company. After a lengthy hearing on December 6, 1935, at which Tom Burns of Burnside Street talked for over an hour, the council agreed to a compromise motion: To refer a $50,000 tax levy to the voters to pay for a survey and an appraisal of the Northwestern properties. If the voters approved the expenditure, a special election would be scheduled for February 1937. The levy was placed on the ballot for the January 31st municipal election that would also present the voters with the new Portland Traction Company franchise and a $300,000 airport bond issue.

Over the next six weeks, the tax levy took a back seat to the other two measures. Mayor Carson provided no leadership either way, while the private utilities conducted an extensive campaign in the newspapers and on the radio. The City Club surprised a number of tax levy proponents by voting against the measure. It was a waste of money, the club declared. The valuations had already been supplied by Public Utility Commissioner Thomas and the Tacoma consulting firm of Harlan & Carey. Commissioner Clyde agreed, but realized that without compromising on the tax levy approach, the council would have proceeded no further. Clyde probably suspected that he was caught in a no-win predicament. It was even conceivable that the utilities had secretly promoted the compromise while overtly opposing it, assuming that the more liberally inclined voters would agree with the City Club position and oppose it.

The debates between the forces of private and public power usually narrowed down to the question of which system provided lower rates to residential consumers. Each side presented its own set of figures. Few would disagree, however, that Portland's private power rates were low as compared with eastern or midwestern cities. The comparisons were always made, as they are today, with municipal operations in Seattle, Tacoma and Eugene. Despite the chamber of commerce figures, the preponderance of data indicated that the municipal operations were indeed cheaper, but not by much. As the consumption rate increased, however, the differential also increased. There were many methods of classifying rates depending upon the nature of the service. Only rarely did either side define the specific bases for its rate computations. A 1977 study by the TVA showed Portland residential rates for 500 Kwh to be 95 percent higher than Seattle's. New York's were 600 percent higher. In the light of history — considering the historical consequences of past decisions — the recent rate comparisons are far more significant. But 40 years ago, the differences did not appear sufficiently great to enough voters to warrant changing the system.

During the debates of the 1930s and 1940s the utilities always added a tax component to their comparative electrical costs. They maintained that taxes were higher in those cities with municipal power systems. But the tax rates that they quoted were not necessarily comparable. Furthermore, the tax question was a phony issue in the first place. The taxes paid by the private utilities were accounted expenses to be included in the rate base and charged to the rate payers. In essence, all rate payers were also taxpayers. In Portland, the consumer was paying his taxes through his utility bill while in Tacoma he was paying his taxes directly. The utilities also argued that for a city to convert to municipal power would reduce needed tax revenues. What was not indicated, however, was that the projected revenue loss nearly equalled the electric charges that the city owed to the private power companies for providing municipal services such as street lighting — charges that would be saved were the city to own its own distribution system.

Regardless of the arguments, the voters soundly defeated the $50,000 tax levy to fund an appraisal of the Northwestern Electric properties. They did approve the $300,000 bond issue for airport land acquisition and they gave Franklin T. Griffith's Portland Traction Company a new 20 year franchise. The following November, while they were joyfully re-electing Franklin D. Roosevelt, the great advocate of public power, Oregon's voters rejected two state Grange initiatives: One to establish a state hydroelectric board; the other to enable the state to enter into the power transmission business with particular attention to rural areas where the private power rates were higher.

IN RETROSPECT

The day after President Roosevelt was overwhelmingly re-elected in November 1936, Governor Charles H. Martin wired him his hearty congratulations. An action of this sort is difficult to appraise historically without seeming cruel. Governor Martin had fought the New Deal's power policies for three years. He had opposed a CVA. He had vetoed the Grange sponsored legislation, forcing the Grange to submit the ill-fated initiative measures to the voters. As Public Utility Commissioner Charles M. Thomas had written to Representative Walter Pierce: ". . . politics are certainly funny . . . . Here I am supporting Roosevelt's power program and am opposed by a man [Martin] who was elected on a program to support the President and then [I was] ordered . . . to fight the President on Bonneville." Needless to say, Thomas soon resigned.

Without strong leadership from the governor or the mayor, little chance existed for either the state or the city to enter the power distribution business. The utilities and their lobbyists were simply too strong and well financed. Furthermore, in Oregon, as opposed to Washington, the Grange and the American Federation of Labor were weak. Outside of Walter Pierce, Ralph Clyde and the newly organized Oregon Commonwealth Federation, a "non-partisan league of progressives" including socialists, there were increasingly fewer voices to warn Oregonians of the future consequences of their actions.

Commissioner Ralph Clyde urged Portlanders to terminate

the Northwestern Electric franchise before it was too late. Clyde clearly saw — and most Portlanders today are experiencing — that cheap Bonneville power would be "hard to get at low cost unless the city owns its own system." Neither the city council nor the voters heeded his advice as the franchise was renewed in August in 1937. When the Bonneville Power Act was passed by Congress in the same month, the so-called "preference clause" was inserted: "[BPA] shall at all times in disposing of electric energy generated at said project, give preference and priority to public bodies and cooperatives." Supported by court decisions, the "preference clause" has assumed an aura of sacredness, not to be tampered with.

Recent attempts by Oregon political leaders and news commentators to play down the state's missed opportunities do not withstand historical scrutiny. The record indicates clearly, that with strong political leadership, Oregon could have joined Washington in the ranks of public power development. It might also be added that strong support from *The Oregonian* 42 years ago could have made a significant difference. In retrospect, one is forced to agree with Ivan Bloch, one of the most experienced electrical engineers in the country and one of the original members of the Bonneville Power Administration staff: "Oregon [and Portland] had its chance 40 years ago and blew it!"

Timber in Oregon

STEVE WOODRUFF

This piece is reprinted from the June 2, 1980 issue of the Portland weekly Willamette Week. *It ran as part of a series on the effect of changes in the timber industry on Oregon's economy. Steve Woodruff is a reporter for the Yakima* Herald-Republic.

It seems like an obvious paradox. Almost a third of Oregon's sawmills have closed recently because of a slump in the national housing market. There are also gloomy predictions of severe shortages in timber supply, a drop of over 20 percent from present harvest levels. Northwest sawmills apparently need all the timber they can get. Yet every year more and more logs cut in the Northwest end up on ships headed for Japan. Last year, a record 3.4 billion board feet of logs, nearly one-fifth of all the timber harvested in Oregon and Washington, was sent overseas.

Millworkers, longshoremen, timber companies, environmentalists and politicians have been bickering over log exports for years. But the rash of mill closures and threats of dwindling timber supplies have given the issue a new urgency and bitterness, as millworkers and timber companies battle over what they see as matters of survival.

On one side are the people who stand to gain from shipping raw logs to sawmills in the Far East — big timber companies, exporting firms, longshoremen and the state of Washington, whose forests provide 75 percent of exported Northwest timber. On the other side are the Northwest's millworkers, led by the 115,000-member International Woodworkers of America;

small timber companies that don't export logs; and, on occasion, environmentalists.

The timber exporters say that Southern lumber mills have taken over the domestic market for lumber and plywood from the Northwest. They say that the American timber industry needs foreign markets to help it survive fluctuations in the domestic housing market when demand for lumber falls off.

George Hess, a Weyerhaeuser log-export manager, says: "If the domestic market becomes better than offshore markets, we'll concentrate domestically." He adds that by helping timber companies stay afloat, log exports have done the Northwest and its inhabitants more good than harm.

The mill workers and their supporters strongly disagree. The unions have no objections to selling American forest products to foreign buyers. They are adamant, however, that the Northwest's shrinking supply of trees be milled in American sawmills, by American workers. "A log sent overseas is a log not manufactured with American labor," says Jim Weaver, Oregon Fourth District congressman, whose southwestern Oregon congressional district has been hit especially hard by mill closures and supply shortages.

The biggest dispute is what Japanese and other foreign buyers who now purchase raw logs would do if American timber companies sold only cut lumber instead of logs. Log-export critics say the Japanese would have no choice but to buy finished products. Japanese forests account for less than 40 percent of Japan's timber needs and American lumber could find an overseas market. Timber industry officials, however, point to differences in Japanese construction methods, their use of metric measurements and other problems, and claim that Japanese buyers won't shift to American lumber if American timber isn't available.

There are also serious questions about how bans and restrictions on log exports will work. Timber companies already are prevented from cutting logs on federal lands and shipping them overseas. But export critics like Weaver insist that millions of board feet of timber cut on federal lands are slipping through because of loopholes in the law.

Mill closures, dwindling timber supply and record numbers of exported logs have heated up the wrangling over log exports. Shipping timber overseas, however, isn't new. Northwest timber companies have been doing it for decades, and have been defending the practice since they began.

But it wasn't until 1962, the year the Columbus Day storm flattened 11 billion board feet of commercial timber in western Washington and Oregon, that log exports became a major issue. That year some 311 million board feet of raw timber was shipped to offshore markets from Washington and Oregon. The following year log exports more than doubled to some 700 milllion board feet. Japanese buyers were greeted warmly by those who owned the damaged timber (Weyerhaeuser and the state of Washington controlled much of it); Northwest mills didn't have the capacity to handle the glut of logs. Even if the milling capacity existed, the housing market was in one of its low cycles and there were few domestic buyers.

However, the newly expanded Japanese market for logs wasn't a one-shot deal. Having found a new source of raw material to supply their own import-dependent lumber industry, the Japanese steadily increased American log purchases throughout the 1960s. Except for a minor lull in 1969, when Japanese housing starts faltered, and in 1971, when strikes halted the flow of logs from West Coast docks, log exports have continued at an ever-increasing clip. Exports passed the one-billion-board-foot mark in 1966, reached just over 2.89 billion board feet in 1978 and peaked at some 3.4 billion board feet last year.

Those exported logs, mostly western hemlock and Douglas fir, brought exporters $1.6 billion last year according to figures compiled by Weyerhaeuser, the country's largest exporter of logs. Last year logs accounted for nearly one quarter of all U.S. forest products shipped overseas, including all the pulp, paper, plywood and lumber sold to all foreign countries.

But what started with acres of trees blown down by the Columbus Day storm has now become a way of life for Northwest timber companies. Rising costs of labor and transportation have cut into their market in the United States. Once the lumberyard of the nation, Northwest sawmills have lost most of the Midwestern, Southern and Eastern lumber markets to Southern mills and Canadian lumber companies.

In 1978, according to C.W. Bingham, Weyerhaeuser vice president, the labor component in lumber production at Southern mills was half that of West Coast mills, and rail and truck costs to Midwestern and Eastern markets are substantially lower for Southern mills than for ones in Oregon and Washington.

For example, the cost of shipping 1,000 board feet of lumber via rail to Chicago from western Washington is just under $70. Mills in Georgia shipping to the same destination are charged about $35. To ship by sea to domestic markets Northwest mills must use American ships as mandated by the federal Jones Act. However, British Columbia may ship lumber aboard less costly foreign vessels. British Columbia's stumpage prices (the prices paid for standing timber) are lower than in Washington and Oregon, and the 85-cents-to-the-dollar exchange rate on Canadian currency makes lumber from Canada a better bargain than most Northwest mills can offer.

And the situation isn't getting better. Lower labor costs and continued increases in fuel costs combine to hone the South's edge on the big-money markets.

The decision by Northwest timber companies to increase shipping of logs across the Pacific instead of competing in the domestic plywood and lumber market has obvious and severe consequences. If logs are cut down, loaded on ships and sent overseas, Northwest sawmills become increasingly obsolete. The International Woodworkers of American calls a ban on log exports from public timber lands one of its highest priorities. Exporting logs, the union insists, exports jobs.

Their assertion gets some backing from figures compiled by

U.S. Forest Service economist David Darr and published as "Softwood Log Exports and the Value and Employment Issues." Darr figures exporting raw logs creates 4.7 hours of employment per 1,000 board feet shipped. That means last year's 3.4 billion board feet put about 7,900 persons to work. However, milling the logs into lumber uses 12.6 work-hours per 1,000 board feet shipped. According to the formula, last year's log shipments would have created as many as 23,000 additional jobs. Manufacturing plywood creates even more jobs at 19.5 work hours per 1,000 board feet.

Rep. Jim Weaver thinks log exports have a direct impact on employment and, he says, as the region heads into a growing shortage of timber, using valuable timber in a way that doesn't create the most employment is unwise.

Weaver's answer is to ban exports of timber cut on federal lands. If log-exporting timber firms can't sell logs overseas, the thinking goes, they'll be forced to sell lumber milled in American sawmills to their foreign customers.

Within the timber industry, at least among the part of the industry that makes money from selling logs overseas, Weaver's solution is "the simplistic explanation." Says Weyerhaeuser's George Hess, "The Japanese aren't going to come back to the United States and say, 'Please sell us lumber made from those logs you won't sell us.' I don't blame labor people for hoping they can make a political decision in this country and have that affect an economic decision in Japan. But it's just not in the cards."

Japan, the largest buyer of American logs, has a flourishing lumber industry of its own with an estimated 23,000 sawmills. The Japanese want logs, not lumber, Hess insists. And Japan is unlikely to put Japanese millworkers out of work to give American millworkers jobs.

American timber companies are also not the only exporters of logs; Japan currently buys only 29 percent of its logs from the United States, most of them from the Northwest. The Soviet Union supplies 15 percent and another 19 percent comes from various countries, including Chile which has recently gained a greater share of the Japanese market.

But the biggest obstacle to increasing American lumber sales across the Pacific is the difference in Japanese and American home-building methods. Since Japanese builders use a sturdier building construction, they need different sizes and lengths in the lumber they use. According to Bob Hunt, who heads a Japanese marketing project for the Portland-based Western Wood Products Association, those differences make any major jump in lumber exports to Japan unlikely in the near future.

American lumber is suited for platform construction, which uses frames of 2-by-4s atop a platform of 2-by-6 floor joists and sheaths them with plywood or other siding. Japanese builders use post-and-beam construction, building a frame of large exposed beams supported by posts and covered with lathe. Post-and-beam homes are supposed to withstand the rigors of Japanese earthquakes and typhoons better than those built to American standards. The Japanese have been building their homes this way for centuries, using different sizes of lumber than that produced in America. Changing these building habits is going to be a slow process, Hunt said. American lumbermen have had limited success convincing builders in Japan to change their architectural style. Last year, some 10,000 of the 1.3 million homes started in Japan used American-style construction and nearly 300 million board feet of Northwest lumber made its way to Japanese markets, 50 percent more than in 1978. While the increase is encouraging and the potential for future increases is promising, Hunt said, the Japanese lumber market still is small potatoes compared with the United States' forest products industry, which exported $6.8 billion in products last year.

It was only two years ago that the Japanese eased a number of barriers to make it easier for American manufacturers to sell lumber in that country. Of greatest importance was a change in Japanese grading standards that had required regrading American lumber stick by stick as it arrived in Japan. And it was only six years ago that platform construction was permitted by Japanese building codes.

But union critics of log exports charge that the big timber-exporting companies haven't really tried hard to pursue the Japanese lumber market. Denny Scott, an economist with International Woodworkers of America, said that the timber companies have refused to adapt to the Japanese specifications. "They've historically taken the position that 'You guarantee us a market for 2-by-4s and we'll guarantee you a supply of lumber.' "

Scott also argues that timber companies aren't inclined to create an overseas market for lumber because of taxation policies that make it more profitable to ship logs than lumber. By exporting through a domestic international sales corporation, a company may defer indefinitely half the normal tax rate on the value of the logs. According to Scott, the tax break does virtually nothing to stimulate domestic lumber production but does encourage overseas log exports.

The high profits to be had from exporting logs haven't escaped the notice of Washington state. Unlike Oregon, a great deal of Washington's productive timber land is owned by the state, not the federal government. And unlike Oregon, California and British Columbia, which all restrict exports of logs cut on state land, Washington aggressively promotes the practice. Nearly 75 percent of all Northwest log exports come from trees cut in western Washington forests. And of all the timber harvested in Washington last year, two-thirds was loaded on ships bound for foreign ports.

The reason for Washington's eager log-exporting policy is simple: money. Revenues from leasing state timber land help support schools and other state-financed institutions. And, according to Washington Department of Natural Resources officials, since log exports bring in more revenue than domestic lumber production, cutting state timber for export is a better use of the trees.

Washington officials answer critics of the log export policy by pointing to timber receipts returned to the Department of Natural Resources for use in forest-management programs. As much as 25 percent of the revenue collected from state timber sales can go back to the department for land management (although the Washington legislature typically allots about half that each year). That money, department foresters claim, has made Washington's forests more productive. Log exports, they conclude, help alleviate the timber-supply problem rather than contribute to it.

Gamscam

GORDON WALGREN AND SPECIAL AGENT HAROLD W. HEALD

The following conversations are from tape recordings made during an FBI investigation of racketeering in Washington state. Two of Washington's top state legislators, Senate Majority Leader Gordon Walgren and Democratic Speaker of the House John Bagnariol, were indicted along with Olympia lobbyist Patrick E. Gallagher on April 17, 1980. They were charged with twenty-nine counts of bribery, fraud, extortion, racketeering and mail fraud. All three were found guilty and sentenced to five years in jail. Appeals are pending.

The tape recordings were made by FBI agents posing as businessmen with organized crime connections. Transcripts of the tapes were entered into the court record.

January 26, 1980
Red Lion Inn, Jantzen Beach, Oregon
Washington's new annual legislative session and political deals: Walgren was running for state attorney general; Bagnariol and Duane Berentson were running for governor.

Heald: Shit, in a lotta ways, the . . . having a session . . .
Walgren: Oh . . .
Heald: . . . helps you a hell of a lot.
Walgren: Absolutely. Absolutely.
Heald: (laughs)
Walgren: The session gave me a forum. If we can come out just halfway clean, I don't care whether they do anything. Just as long as we don't get a bloody nose from the deal, it's got to be a good deal.
Heald: Jeez.

Walgren: And it can't be a long one because people voted it won't be long and so we won't get into that kind of a problem.

Heald: I'll bet . . .

Walgren: The real problem is doing something.

Heald: I'll bet the governor shuddered when that thing was . . .

Walgren: Oh, yeah.

Heald: Put through. Uh?

Walgren: There was a cartoon showing her throwing up the telephone. She . . . she was answering the telephone and she said, "Yes, yes, well, I'm very pleased that the people voted this in. Yes, you know, I supported it." And then it showed her: "God damn!"

(laughter)

Heald: Oh, shit. (laughs) Where do you think . . . say, John [Bagnariol] doesn't get in.

Walgren: Mm hmm.

Heald: Say she does.

Walgren: Mm hmm. We all had a little agreement among all of us — that includes the Republicans. I don't know what kind of an agreement they have with the governor. I got my own (chuckles) deal with the governor. But if . . . if Berentson gets in, and Baggy doesn't, obviously — or if I don't — Berentson, theoretically, is supposed to take care of us.

Heald: Yeah.

Walgren: If Baggy gets in and then Berentson and I don't get in, he's supposed to take care of us, and vice-versa, if I get in, and those two guys don't do it, it's my obligation to see that I get something for those two guys, you know, if they want it.

Heald: But where would . . . say she gets . . . say you get in and she's reelected . . .

Walgren: Mm hmm.

Heald: . . . where the hell is that going to leave us, do you think, chance-wise to, say next year . . .

Walgren: If Baggy goes against her?

Heald: If he . . . and he doesn't make it?

Walgren: Got problems.

CAMPAIGN CONTRIBUTIONS

Walgren: Well, the first thing is that the Congressmen, though, have a real problem because they cannot, by federal law, accept corporate checks. They cannot accept any labor checks. That's why you have the very sophisticated method of giving campaign contributions that has been developed by the Telephone Company and the Boeing Company. One day, if you're a candidate, uh, you'll just receive in the mail about ten or fifteen or twenty checks all made out for X number of dollars and you'll have never known . . . the name down there is somebody you've never heard before in your life. There'll be a little note with 'em that says, uh, uh, "These are employees of the Boeing Company and we hope that you'll respond, ah, with a thank you letter for all of them." That's how they get around it. Now, the state . . . state, uh, campaigns, there is no . . . there is no law against a corporate contribution or a labor union organization. Where I have had some problems is that when I have taken my own campaign funds and made a contribution to a candidate for federal office . . . Do that with, uh, Norm [Dicks]. And somebody said, "Well, you're using obviously corporate funds to do this because you've received corporate funds (unintelligible)." However, I also put some of my own money in there . . .

December 12, 1979
Sea-Tac Red Lion Inn, near Seattle
Politically correct cars

Walgren: I dumped my Audi. I'm about ready to dump my Jaguar.
Heald: Oh, is that right?
Walgren: Yeah. And, uh, I'm going to buy a Volkswagen Dasher . . . .
Heald: (laughs)
Walgren: . . . station wagon. If I'm going to be travelling around the state, I gotta have a place for a bunch of signs and crap in the back end and something that doesn't look quite as . . . .

Heald: Ostentatious.
Walgren: . . . ostentatious.
Heald: Yeah.
Walgren: (laughs)
Heald: I guess, though, John did that with his . . .
Walgren: Mm hmm. Yeah, yes.
Heald: Hiding his Lincolns or something.
Walgren: Everybody's laughing at him.

Coyote on the Columbia

RICK RUBIN

Coyote is a central figure in the mythology of many Northwest native peoples. In the course of his adventures he made the world as the Indians knew it and established rules to live by. These Coyote stories are from Barefoot in Rainy Eden: The Flatheaded Fish-Eating Chinook of the Columbia River, *an unpublished book about the vanished Chinook tribes of the Columbia. The author, Rick Rubin, is a Portland writer and illustrator.*

Coyote as Everyman

Coyote he considers as worthy of his highest respect, despite the ridiculous and lascivious side of his character; and with him he is strongly inclined to identify the Christ of the whites, for both he and Coyote lived many generations ago, and appeared in this world in order to better the lot of mankind.

Edward Sapir, of *Me'nait*

He was just an ordinary sort of fellow: greedy, selfish and dishonest. His lust for the girls was boundless, his gluttony insatiable. He was never much of a hunter, mice and grass-hoppers were his game; he lied, cheated, and stole, was envious, jealous and competitive. More often than not he bungled some important task and the people suffered forever after. Yet, he had to make the world up as he went along, he alone among the animals had no special skill or instinct to guide him, no fang or claw, musk gland or wing, only his curiosity about what would happen if...

Then, in the process of making up the world, he grew to maturity, and became the champion of the people, he slew fearsome monsters, organized chaos, and invented whatever the people would need. Coyote the changer and transformer was himself capable of change. He was the naked one of the animals; he learned and thereby grew.

What a paradox that lean-flanked, squint-eyed, bandy-legged one was. How like a man. Always playing jokes on the creatures, though when the joke was on him he hadn't much of a sense of humor. When he was young he couldn't be trusted, when old he lusted after every woman, even his grandson's wife. He always favored his daughter over his sons, invented incest, suicide and some of the meanest tricks imaginable, he cheated even his own partner in crime and played all manner of cruel pranks for no apparent reason.

The Chinook didn't invent Coyote. From central Mexico to the northern Great Plains, from east of the Rockies all the way to the Pacific, wherever the animal coyote, *Canis latrans*, ran, Coyote was a central character of the mythology. Our word coyote comes from *coyotl* in the *Nahuatl* language, a Uto-Aztecan language of Mexico. He more than somewhat resembled the Fox of European myths, Steppenwolf they sometimes called his cousin on that continent. He was not the largest, strongest, bravest, prettiest or wisest of the animals. Perhaps he was just the one that most seemed man's equal.

The Chinook did not describe him, but their neighbors the Klickitat said he had the head of a man past middle age with grizzled hair and a coyote's body. The animal, sometimes called prairie wolf, is of the dog family, midway in size between red fox and wolf, with yellowish-grey fur and a bushy black-tipped tail, it weighs from twenty to forty pounds and stands about two feet at the shoulders. The Chinook word for coyote was *italapas*, the Tchinouk, Kathlamet, Multnomah and Clackamas called him that, but upriver the Wishram and Wasco said *isku'leye*, from the Sahaptin word.

Myth age Coyote filled the Chinook consciousness even down near the sea, where coyotes were seldom if ever seen. The Tchinouk told many stores of him, though Blue Jay appeared more frequently. Can he have come with the Chinook all the way from ancient times in the Great Basin? Or did those myths filter down the Columbia River after they arrived? From the valley upward he was the central character of far more stories than any other actor. Yet, he was never chief, as he said himself, when he transformed Antelope: "You shall be no chief, you are an animal, your name shall be Antelope. The human beings will be chiefs, some of them. Salmon is chief. Eagle is chief. I am Coyote, I am no chief."

Sudden anger was the worst of his many bad traits; all too often it affected destiny for the worse. Uncontrollable lust and ravenous hunger were close behind. He'd steal glory that belonged to others, his selfishness was unlimited, he didn't know a good thing when he had it. When at last he grew up, however, he began to work altruistically for the good of the people. He became brave, resolute, sensible, resourceful and even successful.

His excrement sisters, who lived in his belly, were his most powerful ally in the Chinook stories. He brought them out to ask them what was happening. At first they always refused to tell, they said he'd only say he knew that all along. When he threatened them with rain they told him what had happened and what it meant. Then he said that was just what he had been thinking already. "His feces spoke thus to him and told him; always were they two, his younger sisters. And then the two jumped up into him; the one threw him down senseless, the other one jumped up into his belly quietly."

They seem no more than a bit of humor to keep the story moving, he sometimes called them his Cayuse sisters. Yet they were a graphic symbol of that marvelous instant of insight we call the intuitive leap, which men sought then as now. Having pondered a problem night and day without success, he happened to be out back squatting and grunting, absorbed completely in emptying his bowels, and suddenly the answer appeared full grown in his head, as do most insights, scientific or otherwise. Thus, the amusing Chinook story device, like many another element in their myths, turns out to be a penetrating insight into human nature.

Coyote even had a private mythological monster of his own, Wala'lap, said to be named for the sound it made. Coyote would warn Racoon or Deer that Wala'lap might eat him, then run ahead to cover himself with ashes or paint, and appear in the trail before his intended victim, leaping from side to side. Coyote did that because he wanted to eat Racoon or Deer. And so he did.

The greatest Coyote story the Chinook told was the epic of how he went up Columbia River. It consisted of a series of tales, each one of which was said to have its location, the telling of which gave not only a history of how the world was changed, but a geography of the Chinook land as well.

The epic began at the sea and the beginning of the world, at birth, before life was possible. At first Coyote did good and bad intermixed, but after a crucial incident he became mature and responsible and after that did nothing but good for the people. It was thus an account of a man's life, his growth to maturity, and in it Columbia River symbolized life itself.

There were many tales, perhaps fifteen or twenty or twenty-five were told in any one village's complete recital of the epic. Such a recitation may have taken two or three nights, maybe even five. It must have been a singular event when told by a gifted story teller. The people travelled far up river or down to hear how Coyote made the world ready for the people to live in, that epic account of a man's life and a river's course and the possibilities of human existence.

What Coyote Did in This Land

Coyote thought: "Let me be on my way, going all over the land." Then he got ready, and off he went.
                                          The Clackamas beginning

At the mouth of Columbia River Coyote encountered Atatalia, who was destroying the people by tying them on a baby board and sending them to drift out to sea with the command "Go forever." After a while the board floated back, nothing but bones were on it. On the shore the people awaited their fate. Coyote said, "I will try that, and soon I will return." She tied him to the board and sent him adrift, saying "Go forever," but the people cried "Come back again." After a while Coyote returned, alive. Then Atatalia was tied to the board and sent off, when the board returned only her bleached bones were on it. The people offered him a wife, but Coyote said, "No, I do not want a wife, I am to travel up the river."

(Thus did the journey commence. Before that life was not possible, everyone died while still on the baby board. Now the people could grow up and populate the land. Someone suggested it was the bar of the Columbia Coyote defeated. Maybe he stayed a while with that wife before he remembered his mission.)

As he was going along he came to a house where a woman lived with her numerous children. "I have come to invite you, the people are dancing," he said. He suggested they practice their dancing first. While she danced, behind her back, Coyote took hold of her children and wrung their necks. When she started to turn around he said, "Dance it right! You might mix up the children." When he had killed all but a few, one squeaked and she turned to see what he was doing, she flew away and her remaining children with her. Coyote announced, "Whenever will Pheasant have a house? You will only fly around, just Pheasant will be your name." Then he cooked and ate those delicious little pheasants.

(It was the dance of life he had invited her to, in order to live the people will kill and eat the children of Pheasant, and the other animals. Had that glutton killed only a few there would have been many more pheasants for the people. She was Pheasant spirit power, her children that kind of bird, her dance taught pheasants how to behave. Perhaps the story also taught the helplessness of a female without a male to protect her.)

Now he came to a house where another woman lived, her daughter was just at puberty. "Her height remains the same, she does not grow," the mother told Coyote. "Long ago when I was only a young man I knew how to cure that," Coyote said. The girl was to go down to the river next day and find a thing growing in the sand there, she was to sit and wriggle and ride on it. Next day Coyote buried himself in the sand, the girl found that thing standing up there, she rode it, but soon Coyote leaped up crying, "I am a man, and you supposed you would copulate on top of me?" He threw her down. When he had finished the girl ran crying to her mother, she told her what he had done, but her mother replied, "Oh, never mind, he caused you to grow."

(What sounds a naughty story of the rape of a young girl is merely Coyote teaching them that when a girl has stopped growing up it is time for her to start growing out. It was her belly the mother was looking at. Thus too Coyote taught the Chinook what position was proper for lovemaking. If mothers were reminded not to be too gullible, so much the better.)

Now Coyote heard that two women had all the fish penned up, none could ascend Columbia River. He tricked them into taking him into their house by turning himself into a baby, he found their pond full of fish. Coyote made digging sticks and bowls, when he was ready he began to dig a trench to let the water and the fish out into the river. As each digging stick broke he started with another. The women discovered his treachery and struck at him, the bowls protected his head. He won the struggle and the fish entered Big River. "It is not right for you to have all those fish penned up in one place," he said. "Things are going to change. There will be other beings here beside you." He transformed those women into swallows, they fly up the river at salmon time.

(Can the Chinook have remembered a time when no salmon ascended Columbia River, a racial memory of the ice age or the Cascade slide? Without fish, life would be hard along Columbia River. This time Coyote acted for the good of all, taught sharing and punished selfishness.)

He encountered mischievous girls who stirred his lust, from the far bank of the river they cried, "Come make love with us,

Coyote." He swam across, but now they were on the other bank. He swam again, but again they were on the far side. Finally he transformed them into birds, such girls would not make men dizzy any more by their teasing.

As he travelled up the river he named the places. From atop the great cliff at *Skolups*, Cape Horn (mile 132), he looked down to see a person catching sturgeon by hand and putting them in a canoe. Coyote went down and stole a fish, the fellow discovered the theft, he swung his finger in a circle until it came to rest where Coyote was hiding behind a tree. He came to shore and Coyote noticed that he had no mouth. Coyote cooked the sturgeon, the man smelled a piece and then threw it away. Now Coyote took a sharp rock and cut where he thought a mouth ought to be, a rush of bad breath came out. They ate the sturgeon together and the man took him to his village, where Coyote cut the mouths of all the people.

(Like the sturgeon, the man's mouth was inadequate, for sturgeon have tiny mouths. The story is typical of Coyote, he stole fish to see what would happen, then did the man a great favor by attacking him with a knife. We can hardly overestimate the kindness of cutting mouths for the belly people. They said the people of that village, *Nimicxa'ya*, just below Beacon Rock [mile 140], had large mouths and were big talkers forever after.)

Now he encountered a man whose feet were tied together, with wood between his legs; he was turning somersaults and landing on his head. Coyote learned that the man's wife was pregnant and he was packing home firewood. Now Coyote showed the man how to make a proper pack, and accompanied him home to find his wife with a swollen finger from which they expected a baby to emerge. Coyote pulled a thorn from her finger and squeezed out pus. "No!" he told them, "Not in this manner is she to become pregnant." He copulated with the woman to show them how, they had a baby which Coyote declared was their own.

(He had encountered people so primitive they didn't know how to carry wood home, or understand sex and its connection to babies. They must have heard that after you stuck something in it swelled up and something came out. Coyote set them straight, but even when he copulated with the man's wife before his very eyes there was no snickering, this time it was altruism, not lust. Nonetheless, the Clackamas identified the village as *Ninuhltidih*, at Hood River [mile 169], and said the people there were shamelessly sexy, for Coyote had taught them how.)

At *Sketcu'txat*, Vancouver (mile 106) Coyote encountered Wolves asleep around their campfire, he pulled their noses and ears out long so people would beware of them. When they awoke they guessed who had done it, for everyone knew that Coyote was going around the land. They in their turn found Coyote asleep and pulled out his ears and nose too, Coyote forever would look like that.

(It is a typical tale of how things got that way. There must have been lots of wolves on the prairie there, or perhaps it referred to the Hudson's Bay Company carnivores of later times.)

At Rooster Rock (mile 131) Coyote encountered a man sitting beside the trail with an enormously long penis wrapped around him like a rope, he was feeding it bits of wood. Coyote watched with interest, then went on. Across Big River he saw unmarried girls bathing, he got an idea and went back and persuaded the man to trade penises. Now Coyote directed it under water across the river to where the girls were swimming, it entered one and stuck fast. They pulled her up on the bank, which pulled Coyote down into the water, before he drowned he shouted across to cut that thing off where it entered her. Then Coyote took it back and exchanged again, he announced that in the future no penis would be so long or eat wood chips.

Now Coyote swam across and made himself look like an old shaman. That girl was sick, Raven tried to doctor her but failed, they came to ask Coyote to cure her. He agreed, but demanded that five unmarried girls carry him, whereupon he fondled each one in turn until she threw him down in disgust. At the sick girl's house he had them build a screen around her bed and invite loud birds to sing, he went inside and doctored the girl by copulating with her. They could not hear her shouts for their singing. Finally Flea crept inside the screen and spied out what was happening. Coyote fled, the people close behind. Her mother, learning that the girl felt better, told her not to complain, "That old man did well to you."

(This most ribald of Chinook stories dealt with the timeless masculine fear that a larger sex organ must be better. Coyote was always envious. It also expressed a healthy distrust of curing shamans; Raven had no idea what was wrong, while Coyote knew all too well, having caused it.)

Next Coyote came to a house where an old woman sat, he asked for something to eat. Her body was covered with slime and pus, she scraped off some and gave him a dish full. Coyote pretended to eat but threw some over his shoulder and hid some in his quiver. He went on, but began to smell something delicious, he ran about shouting, "Wait for me, do not eat all the food, I am hungry," until he realized the smell came from his quiver. He opened it and found savory salmon flesh, he devoured it all and even chewed up his quiver and arrows. He disguised himself and returned to Salmon to get more, but she said, "I don't know what I can give you. Coyote was here not long ago and I fed him my flesh, but he threw it all away." Coyote perceived that she knew who he was and was only teasing him, he cursed her and went on.

(Had that squinty-eyed fool been more appreciative, Salmon would forever after have given freely of her flesh to the people. Because he insulted her gift, men must work for their food. His gluttony was so mindless he gobbled down arrows and all, heedless of the future.)

He came to a big tree with a hole in it, which opened and closed, seemingly at his command. He climbed inside to take a nap but when he awoke the tree stayed closed. He shouted for help, woodpeckers came one by one, when finally one succeeded in making a hole Coyote saw that she was pretty, he reached through to grab her and she flew off. No other bird would come and peck, so Coyote took himself apart, he threw his eyes out first and then the other parts, and put himself back together outside. Buzzard, however, had stolen his unguarded eyes. Coyote found rose hips and substituted those for eyes, he could see just a little.

Now he came to Snail's house, he groped his way inside and fooled her by pretending he could see a nit crawling on the sky. He tricked Snail into trading eyes, forever after she would have weak eyes out on the end of stalks.

(Here Coyote's lack of foresight trapped him, and his lust, caused by his eyes, kept him trapped. The connection between sex and seeing was clear. As the Tchinouk told it, the wind was twisting that hollow tree open and closed, Coyote mistook the wind's power for his own. Next he threw them out first and lost those offending eyes. Perhaps they used the incident to teach the importance of doing things in the proper order? Substituting rose hips explains poor snail, she is gullible and loses by trading, she will forever carry her house on her back, she will think she is getting somewhere but will be the same place.)

He encountered Skunk and admired that notorious farter's anus. He pled with him, "I am just in a dither about your anus. It is something that is so very nice." They exchanged, and Coyote went along *pupupupupu*, enjoying himself, until he found that his new anus scared off a deer he stalked. Coyote returned to exchange again, and foretold Skunk's odorous future.

As he was going along he decided to stop and suck himself. He piled rocks over himself to hide, and vowed all things to secrecy. When he was finished he went down to the river, a canoe was passing and he asked the people what was new. "Yes," they told him, "Coyote was coming along and he covered himself with rocks. He sucked himself. That is the news that is travelling along." Coyote rushed back to find the rocks he had covered himself with split, they had let out the shameful story. Everywhere he went the people were laughing about what he had done. Coyote said, "To be sure, even though it was I myself, the news did come out of there. Now the people are close at hand. Whatever they may do, if they should suppose that other persons will never find out such news, it will come out nevertheless."

(This apparently naughty story is in fact the single most important one in the epic. Until now Coyote has acted capriciously, helping or harming the people seemingly at random. Having been caught at something shameful, he learned that nothing will remain secret, effect will follow cause, and a person will be held accountable for his every action. With this shock of recognition Coyote comes to maturity. From this moment his every act is bent toward the good of mankind. So important was the story that statues were carved to illustrate it, from the side he is sucking, from the front looking up in surprise, caught in the act. They have been called Flute Player, at least three such have been found, there must have been many more. "The Story About Coyote" is supposed to have taken place opposite Mosier, Oregon [mile 175] on the right bank, which shows the Chinook not deficient in geological insight either, for the great uptilt of earth there is the easternmost edge of the Cascade Range, the turning point between mountains and plateau. They called the spot *Idwo'tca*, "story," the rocks are there still. Someone said it was the clouds that spread the story, Coyote forgot to vow them to silence. Note that the Chinook thought the act shameful, but the telling humorous. Unlike ourselves they were not confused by the magic reality of words.)

Next Coyote came to a small river and noticed a falls there, he decided to make it larger so the people could catch fish more easily and create a place for their drying racks. He made a site to dig camas nearby, he made a good place for the people to live, the people's welfare filled his thoughts now.

As he was going along he came to White Salmon River (mile 168) where there was a large village, he asked them to get him water to drink, but they told him they were afraid of the water, no one drank water there. Coyote sent a girl anyway, she screamed in fear and dropped her bucket. He went down to see dog salmon sporting in the water, their open mouths full of teeth. Coyote made a fish spear, when he asked those people for string they gave him strings of dentalia, he had to teach them about that too. He taught them how to catch and cook and eat salmon, and not to be afraid of the water. They offered him wives, but he did not take them.

(Now Coyote was a mature hero, his altruism acted upon him, he took neither money beads nor wives. Those people were naive and inexperienced, they feared even water until Coyote taught them.)

As he was hurrying along he heard that Atatalia and her husband Owl were roasting and eating people. Coyote tied rattles to his legs and went on. When he encountered Atatalia he was frightened, he tried to get away but could not, his legs shook, which made the rattles sound, which attracted the ogress's attention. She wanted to rattle too, he told her he could help her. They went to her roasting pit and he had her smear pitch all over her body and leap into the pit, beside which the people waited to be cooked. He had the people hold her down with forked sticks until she died. When Owl returned Coyote threw ashes on him and transformed him into a bird. Owl's mournful hoot will be an omen of death. They offered him a wife, but after a while he continued on.

(Atatalia's oven was on an island a few miles above the Long Narrows. His way of tricking her into her own oven may remind some of Hansel and Gretel.)

Next he encountered people wearing long poles across their shoulders to keep cracks in the earth from swallowing them. Coyote allowed himself to be swallowed, in the darkness inside the earth-swallowing monster he heard the people groaning. Coyote made a fire, he saw people lying about dead and dying, the monster called out, "Ho, Coyote, I made a mistake about you. Get outside." Coyote said, "Just how could I go outside? You swallowed me." He saw the monster's heart hanging high above, he took a flint knife and cut it off, and the earth-swallowing monster's dying convulsions threw all the people out. They rewarded Coyote with two wives, he stayed a little while, but then he thought, "Oh, I have never sought women, I am merely traveling here and there." He went on.

(Thus did Coyote make the earth itself safe for people to walk on, he could have avoided trouble but offered himself instead.)

People warned him of a river monster living in the Long Narrows that swallowed people. Coyote went along taunting the monster, "Itci'xyan, swallow me!" until finally the river spirit did so. Now Coyote found himself in a dark empty place. "People, build a fire and I'll stay all night," he said. He lighted a fire and found the people and their canoes lying about; high above beat the monster's heart. Itci'xyan realized his mistake. "Come out, Coyote," he said, "I didn't mean to swallow you." "How can I come out?" said Coyote. "There is no door." He built a ladder of canoes and cut Itci'xyan's heart with his flint knife. He had the people sit in their canoes, when the heart fell free a great breath blew all the people out. Then Coyote announced that in the future a person might drown once in a while but the river spirit would not kill everyone like that.

(Thus did Coyote tame the mighty Columbia's most powerful spirit, who elsewhere conferred gambling power and gave his daughter and great wealth to an abandoned boy. In one version they offered Coyote ten wives, but though he stayed a while, he did not keep them.)

Now he encountered a monstrous mountain that sucked in birds or anything, the monster tried to breathe Coyote in, but he tied himself to another mountain and challenged the monster. They battled back and forth by sucking in breath, at last the monster's belly burst.

(Thus the third monster: now Coyote had made earth, water and air safe for the people. Coyote did not go inside the sucking monster, so we do not know what the inside of one of those looked like.)

Now Coyote came to *Sk'in*, the first Sahaptin village above the Chinook. He saw that the people there did not act right, they had foolish ways and all wanted to be chiefs at once. "It is not right that these people should be so proud," he said, "I will humiliate them." He climbed up on the rocks behind the village and pissed upon them. He went across to Celilo falls and instructed the people there what do to, he named them *Ilka'imamt*.

(Thus did Coyote define the eastern frontier of Chinook *Illahee*, noting that the people there spoke differently and had foolish ways. No doubt the Sahaptin speakers told the story differently.)

Now Coyote reached the Sun, he offered to be her slave, he would follow her about and work for nothing. She let him come along, they crossed the sky together. Coyote saw everything, the way the people were acting, how women were eloping and things were being stolen and people killed. He shouted, "I see what you people are doing." Again, another day they went and again he saw and cried out, and then the Sun told him, "You are too mean. It would not be good that you should always tell on people, there would be trouble." It is because of this that people do not find out everything, if Coyote had become the Sun no one would have had any secrets. Then Coyote stopped, he gave it up, he had come to the end.

(Thus, one final flaw of Coyote's: having become good, he became too good. He was prevented from having the power of the Sun lest the world become unliveable in another way. If this seems to conflict with "The Story About Coyote," well, life is full of contradictions, and so are myths.)

"This is the story of Coyote. Thuswise did the men of old in ancient days relate the tale. Today there are no longer such men of old."

Series Index

THE NORTHWEST EXPERIENCE 1, June 1980
THE NORTHWEST EXPERIENCE 2, May 1981

Hill, Greg, *Energy 1990*, a condensed version of *The Politics of Energy 1990*, 1978.
NWE 2, pp. 104-140

Honig, Doug, and Victor Steinbrueck, "Victor Steinbrueck," an expanded version of the interview, "Planning for Lovers and Friends," which appeared in the *Seattle Sun*, May 14, 1980.
NWE 2, pp. 25-33

Lewis, Linda, "Ocean Ranching," reprinted from the Seatle *Post-Intelligencer*'s Sunday magazine, *P-I/Northwest*, June 17, 1979.
NWE 2, pp. 51-63

MacColl, E. Kimbark, "Bonneville," excerpted from *The Growth of a City: Power and Politics in Portland, Oregon, 1915 to 1950*, The Georgian Press, 1979.
NWE 2, pp. 141-153

McNulty, Tim, "Myths and a Sense of Place," essay and poem (Bodhidharma Crossing the Graywolf on a Ry-Krisp), reprinted from *Truck 18*, 1978.
NWE 1, pp. 136-138

Manning, Harvey, "Walking the Beach," excerpted from a work in progress, *Walking the Beach to Bellingham*, 1981, to be published by Madrona Publishers.
NWE 2, pp. 3-13

Morgan, Murray, "Laying Out Tacoma," excerpted from *Puget's Sound*, University of Washington Press, 1979.
NWE 1, pp. 13-19

Mungo, Raymond, "Charity Begins at Home," on Seattle houses, excerpted from *Cosmic Profit*, The Atlantic Monthly Press, 1980.
NWE 1, pp. 99-109

Neil, J.M., "Parks for Profit and Pleasure," 1980.
NWE 1, pp. 3-10

Oregon Legislative Research, Beverly March, "Oregon's Legislative Innovations," a report to the Oregon Legislative Assembly, 1975.
NWE 2, pp. 100-103

Oregon Legislative Research, Bob Grundstad, "Ballot Slogans," excerpted from a report to the Oregon Legislative Assembly, 1978.
NWE 1, pp. 35-38

Pintarich, Dick, "The Portland that Might Have Been," reprinted from *Oregon Magazine*, August 1979.
NWE 1, pp. 20-34

Portland, City of, "Residential Displacement in Portland," report summary, 1979.
NWE 1, pp. 110-113

Rabinowitz, Alan, " 'The Housing Situation' and 'The Housing Market,' " 1980.
NWE 1, pp. 77-90

Rubin, Rick, "Coyote on the Columbia," Chinook Indian mythology, excerpted from an unpublished work, *Barefoot in Rainy Eden*, 1980.
NWE 2, pp. 166-179

Sale, Roger, "J.C. Olmstead in Seattle," excerpted from *Seattle, Past to Present*, University of Washington Press, 1976.
NWE 1, pp. 11-12

Scribner, Peter, *An Ecocity for Puget Sound*, excerpted from a master's thesis in Urban Planning at the University of Washington, 1971.
NWE 1, pp. 155-180

Seattle, City of, "Seattle Displacement Study," excerpted from a report on housing and neigh-